THE CV COACH

Hilton Catt and Patricia Scudamore

First published in Great Britain in 2014 by Hodder & Stoughton. An Hachette UK company.

First published in US in 2014 by The McGraw-Hill Companies, Inc.

British Library Cataloguing in Publication Data: a catalogue record for this title is available from the British Library.

Library of Congress Catalog Card Number: on file.

10 9 8 7 6 5 4 3 2 1

Typeset by Cenveo® Publisher Services.

Printed and bound in Great Britain by CPI Group (UK) Ltd, Croydon CR0 4YY.

Hodder & Stoughton policy is to use papers that are natural, renewable and recyclable products and made from wood grown in sustainable forests. The logging and manufacturing processes are expected to conform to the environmental regulations of the country of origin.

Hodder & Stoughton Ltd

338 Euston Road

London NW1 3BH

www.hodder.co.uk

Also available in ebook

CONTENTS

MEET THE COACHES

Patricia Scudamore and **Hilton Catt** have 35 years' combined experience of interviewing and preparing candidates. Between them they bring the perspective of both recruiter and interviewee. From backgrounds in HR management, they set up their own business in 1988 and began writing on careers subjects 15 years ago. They have now written more than 20 books based on their experience of what it takes to make careers work in today's rapidly changing and uncertain world.

Patricia and Hilton were among the first to embrace the idea of people taking on the job of managing their own careers as opposed to leaving it to employers to do the thinking for them. They have seen for themselves the richness and diversity modern careers can offer and one of the recurring themes in their work is exploiting this richness and diversity to the full. They view writing books as the best way to spread their messages to the greatest number of people. Their other books in the Teach Yourself series include *Successful Career Change In A Week* (2013), *Successful Cover Letters In A Week* (2013) and *Successful Job Applications In A Week* (2012).

HOW TO USE THIS BOOK

 OUTCOMES FROM THIS CHAPTER

- Understand the importance of the CV in the contemporary job market and how this has come about.

- Appreciate the key features of this book and how to make it work for you.

- Begin to think about your attitude towards CVs in general and your own CV in particular by undertaking your first 'coaching session' – a simple questionnaire.

Those of you who are old enough can probably remember a time when most people didn't have CVs. The standard way to apply for a job was to write a letter in which you gave details of your education, qualifications, work experience and so on, along with information to explain why the position interested you. Sometimes this did the trick and you got a letter back asking you to attend an interview. Sometimes the employer sent you an application form to fill in first.

CVs in the early days tended to feature only at the very top end of the job market – for example senior management positions in top companies. Even here, it was not unusual to find that the CVs in question had been prepared not by the people concerned but by the consultants who had been retained to advise on the appointment. It was a way of parading the candidates they had sourced to their clients, and it looked good or, more to the point, it made the candidates look good (and, on occasions, better than they really were). However, it wasn't long before everyone got in on the act to the extent that, today, someone who doesn't have a CV is a comparative rarity. In most cases the reason for this is either that they haven't been active on the job scene for a number of years or, for one reason or another, they are complete newcomers to the world of work.

THE CV REVOLUTION

So what brought about the big change? What made it possible for more and more people to aspire to having a professional-looking CV? The answer is to be found in two late twentieth-century developments:

- **the growth in home PC ownership** and the availability of relatively low-cost, high-quality inkjet or laser printers

- **the advice now widely available on how to produce a CV** – advice that comes in the form of numerous books on the subject, tips and even ready-made CVs that can be downloaded from the Internet, not to mention people like outplacement counsellors and the support provided by bodies such as public employment services.

Yet with the good also comes the bad. While, on the face of it, there's nothing wrong with standard templates, they can and do introduce an unfortunate tendency for everyone's CV to look the same. Where the idea is to make your CV stand out from all the others, this sameness works against you – a point you need to consider when you're attacking competitive job markets and one that will come up again as you work your way through the book.

The other factor that has a big bearing on the spread of CVs is the way employers deal with job applications. This has changed since the days when the ad invited you to write in with details of your age, qualifications and work experience. Now most of these ads ask for a CV, so, if you don't have one, you will be faced with a problem straight away. The first port of call for people who are embarking on a journey into the job market, therefore, is to get a CV prepared or, as is more often the case, to bring the one they've already got up to date.

What other reasons could there be for needing a CV? CVs are normally seen in the context of making job applications, but this isn't the whole story. For example, self-employed people who are trying to source work are sometimes asked to submit a CV as evidence of their skills and competence. What this serves to demonstrate is that CVs are there to do what you want them to do and this is a central message of this book.

WHAT'S IN IT FOR *YOU*?

So, assuming that you're like most people and you've already got a CV, two questions will be figuring in your thoughts as you pick up this book and start to read it:

1. Am I going to learn anything new?

2. How will this knowledge benefit me?

The book is a mixture of interactive exercises ('coaching sessions') and commentary text. The exercises are not just there to make you think. The idea is to involve you in the process of acquiring a better understanding of the subject matter by relating it to your own thoughts and experiences.

Each chapter has the following features:

 OUTCOMES FROM THIS CHAPTER

A bullet list at the start of each chapter sets out exactly what you will have got from that chapter by the time you have finished it. This is in terms of both what you will have *learned* (e.g. from the running text) and what you will have *done* (e.g. in the 'coaching sessions').

 COACHING SESSIONS

These are the key, meaty features within each chapter that will get you really working on, and interacting with, the ideas given in the commentary text. They include self-assessments, checklists and reflective questions.

 COACH'S TIPS

These are key, 'snappy' pieces of advice, often drawn from our own experience.

 NEXT STEPS

This section is an end-of-chapter bullet list summarizing what you have learned and placing that learning in the context of the chapters that follow.

TAKEAWAYS

Reflective questions at the end of each chapter will help you focus on how what you have read and done in that chapter has helped you, *personally*.

What counts at the end of the day, after all, is what *you* get out of the book, what you take away with you when you've finished reading it, and how much of what you've learned is information you can use.

The book therefore starts with the all-important task of deciding what task you want your CV to perform. Do you want to use it, for example, to attack overcrowded areas of the job market where competition from other candidates is going to be the biggest concern? Or are you thinking about sending off a mailshot to selected employers in the hope they might have something suitable for you? Once you've decided the aim, you can turn your thoughts to what needs to go in your CV and what, in some cases, to leave out.

As soon as you've got your CV down on paper, you can start to look at putting it to use, remembering all the time that a CV is only any good if it gets you the result you want. By following the advice in this book, you will be able to create a great CV ready to tailor to all your job applications.

! COACH'S TIP

Know your aim

First decide the aim, then design a CV that will achieve the aim.

⍥⍥ COACHING SESSION 1

CVs: myth or reality?

Here is a list of ten statements that represent commonly held opinions about CVs and how they should be written. In each case say whether you agree with the statement or not by ticking the appropriate box.

You can look at the list again when you have finished reading the book. It will help you to see where your ideas may have changed.

Agree/Disagree

1. A CV is there to get you interviews. ☐ ☐
2. A CV is no good without a good cover letter. ☐ ☐
3. CVs that are more than three pages long don't get read. ☐ ☐
4. A CV with your photograph on the front page makes more impact. ☐ ☐
5. Missing out blemishes from your past is all part of the game. ☐ ☐
6. A good CV is one that is relevant to the job for which you're applying. ☐ ☐
7. CVs designed by experts are better than ones you put together yourself. ☐ ☐
8. CVs full of spelling mistakes automatically get binned. ☐ ☐
9. CVs are rarely read from start to finish. ☐ ☐
10. Your CV should be seen as an extension of your personality. ☐ ☐

WHAT DO YOU WANT YOUR CV TO DO?

✔ OUTCOMES FROM THIS CHAPTER

- Understand why it is important to define the task you want your CV to perform.
- Consider the part your CV plays in making a good first impression.
- Know what readers of your CV want to see.
- Understand why being concise matters.
- Recognize what it takes to be 'employer-friendly'.

DEFINING THE TASK YOU WANT YOUR CV TO PERFORM

Ask a cross-section of people what a CV is for and it's a safe bet that most of them will answer, 'To get you interviews.' But think again. To help stimulate your thoughts, here is a coaching session for you to try.

𝒬𝒬 COACHING SESSION 2

What's a CV for?

Consider these four people who all need a CV but for different reasons:

Brooke is looking to make a big step forward in her career and needs a CV to apply for top-drawer jobs she sees advertised on websites and in leading national newspapers.

Caspar is a sales high-flier looking for more money. He wants a CV to send out to six of his firm's leading competitors to see whether any of them would be prepared to meet his aspirations.

Tim has a job that is at risk following the merger of his firm with one of its biggest rivals. Tim needs a CV to register with three agencies that specialize in people like him.

Steffi works for herself and has been asked to provide a CV by a prospective client.

In each of these four cases, what is the task that the CV has to perform?

Brooke:

_____

_____

_____

_____

Caspar:

_____

_____

_____

Tim:

_____

_____

_____

Steffi:

_____

_____

_____

_____

A 'one size fits all' approach to designing a CV doesn't work. What you need to do before you give any thought to 'putting pen to paper' is to decide what you want your CV to do for you. Brooke, for example, needs a CV that will be capable of taking on and overcoming the high-powered competition she will undoubtedly come up against as she strives to climb the management ladder. Caspar, on the other hand, has no worries about competition. What his CV has to do is connect him with jobs that pay more money.

The four cases in Coaching session 2 are not an exhaustive list. Take, for example, someone who needs a CV to help them make a change of career. Among the needs here will be to convince readers that:

- they've thought it through properly
- they're serious.

THE IMPORTANCE OF FIRST IMPRESSIONS

You won't often be in situations where the recipient of your CV will be someone who knows you or who knows you through a third party. In most cases, your CV and the cover letter that goes with it will be an important first impression.

First impressions are important because:

- good or bad, they tend to stick
- once they're formed, they're very hard to shift.

First impressions have an important part to play in job applications and how far an application will go. A CV that makes a good first impression should pave the way to an interview. On the other hand, one that makes a bad first impression is almost certainly destined to find its way to the reject pile.

COACHING SESSION 3

Put yourself in an employer's shoes...

Imagine that you've been given the job of going though a batch of CVs that have arrived in response to an ad you have placed. In terms of presentation, what would make a good first impression with you and, conversely, what would act as a turn-off?

In candidate selection, the **halo effect** describes the tendency to see some good points in a candidate at the beginning of the process and, thereafter, to ignore any flaws that come to light. The halo effect can also work in reverse. Bad points at the beginning can overshadow good points that come out later on.

HOW A GOOD CV CAN GO ON WORKING FOR YOU

The job of your CV isn't done when you get the letter, email or phone call inviting you to come in for an interview. It can and does go on working for you – this subject is explored in more detail in Chapter 8. However, just as a taster, consider that when you arrive for an interview you will probably find the interviewer seated behind a desk with your CV and cover letter in front of him or her. In this way, your CV and cover letter become the starting point for the interview and go on to play a large part in determining:

- the **direction** the interview takes
- the **topics** that come up for discussion
- the **questions** that are asked.

THE STANDARD OF ENGLISH

Many employers automatically bin CVs they receive that contain spelling mistakes, bad grammar or apostrophes in the wrong place.

COACHING SESSION 4

Your CV and the standard of English

What are your thoughts on poor standards of English in CVs? Think back to the last CV you wrote: what steps did you take to check the spelling, punctuation and grammar?

_____

_____

_____

_____

_____

_____

_____

_____

Take responsibility for the quality of the image you project

It is important that anything you put in a CV (or a cover letter) projects an image that is consistent with the one you want to project. Above all, don't be seen as someone who is careless or lacks the capacity to pay attention to detail. Sadly, however, this is how a CV with mistakes will come across. To an employer, the person who put it together clearly couldn't be bothered to check it properly and this doesn't say a lot for how the same person would get on when given some real responsibilities.

There is more on making sure that the English in your CV is up to scratch in the final chapter of this book.

COACH'S TIP

Get noticed for the right reasons

The idea is to catch the reader's attention because of what you have to offer in terms of your skills and abilities, not your bad grammar and spelling mistakes.

Does it make sense?

The syntax in some CVs is so bad that the content doesn't make sense and these CVs are binned for that reason alone. Employers are sometimes faced with dozens, if not hundreds, of CVs, so the time they spend on reading each one is strictly limited. When they come across a CV where it's unclear what the candidate meant, the natural inclination is to pass it by. Often, a bit more care would have been all it would have taken to see the problem and do whatever was necessary to put it right.

PRESENTATION

The appearance of your CV will clearly have a major impact when it lands on someone's desk. Will this impact be a good one or will its appearance let you down?

The following coaching session is a useful checklist of dos and don't about presentation. Keep it handy and refer to it when you are preparing your next CV.

COACHING SESSION 5

CV presentation: dos and don'ts

Here is a list of dos and don'ts for you to go through. Make a note of any that you may want to go back to later.

- **Do** use black ink on standard A4 white paper. This is because, on some part of its journey, your CV may have to be copied and/or run off on a black-and-white printer. Grey on grey doesn't reproduce well.

- **Do** stick to conventional fonts of the kind you normally find used in business correspondence, e.g. Arial or Times New Roman.

- **Don't** use strange fonts or graphics because you think they will look different and catch the eye. They will catch the eye, but not in the way you hope. Strange fonts and graphics tend to go with strange people.

- **Don't** try to save space or get more on the page by using font sizes that will have your readers reaching for their glasses (or, conversely, not bothering).

- **Do** take care when printing off, especially on inkjet printers where blots and smudges can become a problem.

- **Don't** print off your CV using a cartridge that's on its last legs or, worse still, use a ball-point pen to ink in any parts that haven't come out very well.

- **Do** make sure that every CV you send out is in pristine condition.

- **Don't** recycle CVs. If one is returned to you, bin it straight away.

- **Do** be careful where you store your printer paper. A waft of stale cigarette smoke or the smell of last night's fry-up as your CV comes out of the envelope won't make a good first impression.

- **Do** use a standard white A4 envelope if you're sending your CV in the post.

- **Don't** fold your CV to make it fit into a small envelope. It will forever bear the crease marks and, more to the point, it introduces the risk of someone at the other end with a not-too-clean pair of hands trying to smooth it out.

- **Do** stick to the default settings built into your computer software when it comes to determining the width of the margins or the spaces at the tops and bottoms of pages.

- **Don't** try to cram more in by using every centimetre of space available.

- **Don't** hand-write your CV (some people still do). It looks old-fashioned but, more to the point, you lose the capacity to edit, make corrections and run off drafts.

WHAT MAKES YOUR CV INTERESTING?

When someone picks up your CV, will they find it interesting or, more to the point, will they find it interesting enough to want to go on reading it from start to finish?

⚆⚆ COACHING SESSION 6

Your CV and your audience

Put yourself in an employer's shoes. What would you be looking to see in a CV? What would catch your eye and make you focus your interest?

_____

_____

_____

_____

_____

_____

_____

_____

_____

_____

The reader of your CV is the person you need to consider – no one else. For example, what you find interesting about yourself and what employers with vacancies to fill would find interesting are often two completely different things. Employers will be looking for people who tick the boxes in terms of their skills, experience, qualifications and possibly a few other attributes. When you have some or all of these attributes, these are known as your **key matches**, and these key matches, providing they are given sufficient prominence in your CV, are what will catch employers' eyes and make them keep reading. Anything else in your portfolio will largely be seen as background material and, while not entirely irrelevant, will certainly have secondary importance.

THE IMPORTANCE OF CUSTOMIZING CVS

All employers are different, so what one employer sees as an essential requirement for a job won't necessarily be viewed in the same way by another. When thinking about the task you want your CV to perform, a CV you put together to apply for Job A won't be one you can use again when it comes to applying for Job B.

 COACH'S TIP

Customize, customize, customize!

Although the message about customizing CVs has been out there for some time, it is still surprising how many people use the same CV every time they apply for a job. The impression this gives to employers is that the applicant couldn't be bothered to go to the trouble of putting together a new one. This is hardly a recipe for success!

A warning

Where large numbers of CVs are being processed, the job of sorting out those that are of interest from those that are not is sometimes done by computer, using software programmed to search for key words and phrases. This is where a CV that makes no attempt to bring into prominence what the candidate has to offer in terms of the requirements of the job can become an early casualty. The CV gets put on the reject pile without ever being seen by human eyes.

WHY BEING CONCISE MATTERS

A great deal has been written about the need to keep CVs concise. However, achieving conciseness is challenging and can sometimes come into conflict with the need to say all you want to say about yourself.

The 'one quick read' test

Especially in situations where your CV is going to be one of many that an employer receives, it has to stand up to some pretty robust treatment. Notably:

- it may not be read from start to finish
- it will rarely be read twice (once on the reject pile it will tend to stay there).

A CV that is concise will have more chance of surviving this treatment than one that isn't.

COACHING SESSION 7

Achieving conciseness

What are your thoughts on the ideal length for a CV? What, in your opinion, would be the risks if a CV exceeded the ideal length?

_____

_____

_____

_____

_____

_____

_____

_____

_____

_____

_____

_____

_____

_____

_____

_____

How to achieve conciseness

Don't try to achieve conciseness by trying to cram everything into the smallest space possible. People who do this usually resort to:

- using ridiculously small and reader-unfriendly font sizes
- reducing the width of margins
- not leaving spaces between sections and paragraphs.

The result in most cases is something that looks a mess and scores a bad first impression.

Conciseness is best achieved by ensuring that everything you say in a CV is **relevant** to the position for which you are applying – that is, relevant to the task you want it to perform. Irrelevant information should be left out and anything on the borderline should be given the briefest mention possible.

AN EMPLOYER-FRIENDLY CV

In the context of CVs, being employer-friendly means doing all you can to make your CV a quick and interesting read. Employers, particularly those faced with a big pile of CVs to get through, will want to find the fastest route possible to deciding whether you're someone they want to interview or not. You can assist them in this process by highlighting the matches between:

■ what you have to offer

■ the requirements of the job.

Their attention is drawn straight away to what matters most, and by doing this you leave nothing to chance or to a tired pair of eyes failing to pick up what's buried in a lot of otherwise irrelevant information.

NEXT STEPS

Chapter 1 has been about examining the task you face when you sit down to the job of designing a CV. The key points are that:

- no one single CV is going to perform all the tasks

- to be any use, a CV has got to be capable of performing the task for which you intend it.

CVs and the cover letters that go with them can play a big part in making a good first impression on people who are going to be important in determining the directions you go in next in terms of your career. You need therefore to be confident that your CV will do what you want it to do when it reaches its recipient.

In the next chapter you will be looking at putting your CV to work and what you need to include in it to get the result you want.

TAKEAWAYS

Has reading this chapter taught you anything new about customizing CVs? Is there anything in particular that you found useful?

_____

_____

_____

_____

_____

_____

_____

_____

_____

What do you plan to do differently when you next need to put together a CV? List the main points here.

_____

_____

_____

_____

_____

_____

_____

_____

_____

_____

_____

Are you satisfied that you are doing all you can to avoid spelling and grammatical mistakes? If you think you can do better, what plan of action have you come up with?

_____

_____

_____

_____

_____

_____

_____

_____

_____

Have you learned anything useful about how to achieve conciseness? As a result of reading this chapter, do you think that your previous attempts at designing CVs may have failed the 'one quick read' test? Write some notes here on what you plan to do in future to rectify this problem.

_____

_____

_____

_____

_____

_____

_____

_____

_____

_____

_____

Have you had any thoughts about how you could make your CVs more interesting for the people who have to read them?

_____

_____

_____

_____

_____

_____

_____

_____

_____

_____

_____

What do you think you have learned about using your CV to make a good first impression? How will this knowledge benefit you?

_____

_____

_____

_____

_____

_____

_____

_____

_____

_____

_____

_____

2 PUTTING YOUR CV TO WORK

✔ OUTCOMES FROM THIS CHAPTER

- Know how to use your CV to communicate your ambitions.
- Understand the benefits for you of making it clear where you're coming from and what you're seeking to achieve.
- Know what to do to avoid interviews that will go nowhere.
- Understand the importance of presenting yourself in a way that is a true reflection of who you are and what you can do.

COMMUNICATING THE MESSAGE

A good CV is one that:

- makes your ambitions clear to anyone who reads it
- leaves no room for misinterpretations.

🗩🗩 COACHING SESSION 8

Sending the wrong message

Consider the following case study. It illustrates what can happen when the recipient of someone's CV picks up the wrong messages.

Case study: Jo

Jo works in sales for a distributor of imported food products. Jo is 27 and she has been in her job for four-and-a-half years. Jo's problem is money: she thinks that she is not being paid enough. Two months earlier she had presented a case for a salary increase to her boss Cindy, the National Sales Manager. Cindy, however, was unreceptive, telling Jo that she would have to wait until business took a turn for the better. She also told Jo that in the current climate there was no scope for sanctioning pay rises.

Dissatisfied with this reply, Jo has now decided to try her luck on the job market. Her thoughts turn to her CV, which she last updated when she was applying for her current position. She is pleased to see that her CV doesn't need to have many changes made to it. Her employment history needs to be brought up to date, of course, and some of her contact information has changed, but that is it. Ten minutes' work and her CV is all ready to go out.

Over the next few weeks, Jo keeps a careful eye on jobs she sees advertised in trade journals and on websites. In most cases, she notices that the ads don't go into detail about salary. They use words such as 'attractive', 'competitive' or 'negotiable', but Jo sees no problem with this because she is certain that she is seriously underpaid.

Jo sends her CV off to five companies she picks out – companies advertising for experienced sales executives with proven track records in selling to the retail sector. As a result of her efforts, she is invited to attend three interviews but this is where she hits a problem. The interviews are all in normal office hours, which leaves Jo with the task of thinking up three different excuses for taking time off work. She puts these excuses to Cindy, but, while Cindy agrees, Jo can tell she is suspicious.

All three interviews follow a similar pattern. On the face of it, they go well but when Jo asks for information on salary she is given the answer that the package will be discussed at a later stage.

A few days pass and then, for one of the jobs, Jo receives an email asking her to a second interview, again during office hours. She asks Cindy for more time off, but on this occasion she is met with a barrage of questions. Cindy demands to know what's going on and adds that Jo seems to be letting her private life get in the way of her work. Jo somehow manages to bluff her way through, but she is left with the distinct feeling that there will be trouble if she has to ask for any more time off.

The second interview goes as well as the first. Jo waits for the subject of salary to come up but it doesn't and the interview ends with the interviewer promising he will get back to her within the next few days. Sure enough, the call comes through. Jo has got the job, she is told, and, as far the salary is concerned, the company will match what she is being paid now with the promise of a review at the end of the year providing trading conditions remain favourable. What does Jo think? Joe is not sure what to say. Her only reason for looking for another job was to earn more money, not to make a sideways move. Jo explains the situation and asks whether the offer can be improved. The answer to this is no. Matching her current salary is as far as the company is prepared to go. Jo asks for 24 hours to think it over but she knows she has already made her mind up. It would be foolish to change jobs for no gain. However, what bothers Jo most is that, if she is going to pursue her ambitions any further, it will mean asking for more time off work to go to interviews. It will lead to friction with Cindy, she is sure of it.

What are your thoughts on this case study? What could Jo have done to avoid the situation she has found herself in?

_____

_____

_____

_____

_____

_____

_____

_____

_____

_____

_____

_____

Define the aim

Going back to what you learned in Chapter 1, the first job when you design a CV is to decide what you want it to do for you. In Jo's case, she wanted a CV to help her find a better-paid job. However, what appears to have been the problem with the updated version of her old CV is that it didn't make it clear that this was the aim. If she had made it clear, then the recipients of her CV would have seen for themselves where her ambitions lay.

If, like the company who made her the offer, they couldn't come up with the level of salary she was seeking, they would not have invited her to the interview in the first place and the conflict with Cindy would not have arisen. More to the point, perhaps, Jo would have been able to keep the time she could take off work without being asked awkward questions for other, more potentially worthwhile interviews (interviews with employers with fewer constraints on their purse strings).

Have an aim with a positive outcome

This is important. People have a tendency to define their aims in negative terms. Here are a few examples:

All these negative statements may be true for these people, but the sentiments expressed don't define the paths these employees want their futures to follow or the messages they want their CVs to deliver.

COACHING SESSION 9

Positive messages

Can you do better? Using the blank speech bubbles below, see what you can do to turn each of the above negative thoughts into positive ones.

COACH'S TIP

Be unambiguous

Someone picking up your CV needs to understand in clear and unambiguous terms:

* where you're coming from
* what you're seeking to achieve.

Take responsibility

Going back to the case study, the employer who put Jo through two interviews without broaching the subject of salary must share some of the blame for wasting her time and theirs. After all, they were running the show. However, apportioning the blame isn't the issue. Jo found herself in hot water with her boss over the time she was taking off work, so, if she is going to carry on looking for a better-paid job, she needs a way of making sure that any interviews she goes to in future are with employers who can fulfil her ambitions.

So what's the answer? It is this: Jo has to take ownership of the job of communicating the message about where she's coming from and what she's seeking to achieve. In turn, this means not relying on employers to do the job for her by trying to read between the lines of her CV.

HOW TO MAKE SURE YOUR AIMS ARE UNDERSTOOD

So how do you go about making sure that your aims are understood by anyone picking up your CV? How do you make sure that the interviews you're invited to are the right ones?

COACHING SESSION 10

Assess your CV: are the aims transparent?

Get out the last CV you put together. Would someone reading it be able to see your aims at a glance? In terms of getting the message across clearly, what would you do now that might make your aims and ambitions more transparent? Record your answer here.

_____

_____

_____

_____

_____

_____

Start with a clean sheet

Jo is a good example. When she had a need for a CV, she got out the last one she put together and looked for where the information in it needed to be brought up to date – and, to be fair to Jo, this is probably the way most people would have proceeded. What the case study doesn't tell us is whether or not her old CV had a section setting out her aims and ambitions. What is almost certain, though, is that her current aims and ambitions would be different from the ones she had had four-and-a-half years earlier.

 COACH'S TIP

Start afresh

While some of the information in a CV doesn't change significantly from one year to the next, a lot does, so in many ways it is easier to set about the task of preparing a CV with almost a blank page in front of you. Not only do you avoid repeating the mistakes you made in the past, but you can also bring in new experience – underlining the fact that the writing of a CV is something you get better at.

People often spend hours in front of the screen tweaking and twiddling old CVs. Harmless enough, you may think, but one of the unfortunate side effects of this tweaking and twiddling is that the CVs in question get longer and the information in them increasingly complicated and, for this reason, open to misunderstandings. The main reason, however, for advising you to start with a clean sheet is so that you can be sure that everything you put in the CV is **relevant** to the job for which you are applying and you won't inadvertently be bringing in messages that were relevant only to a job you applied for in the past.

Don't leave the employer to guess what's driving you

Jo needs to get into her CV her reason for looking for another job, which is to earn more money. In a prominent place, therefore, she needs to say what she is earning now and that she is looking for an improvement. Employers who pick up her CV will then be clear about:

- how much they will have to offer her to move
- whether or not they can afford her.

Other people will have different aims from Jo, different messages they need to get across on their CV. For example, someone looking for a job where they can use their language skills will need to make this clear.

Always set out your pay expectations

No one needs reminding that money is an important issue and, even though it may not be the main reason why you are looking for another job, there is still a minimum figure you will need to earn to keep the wolf from the door and buy whatever it is you've become accustomed to. Again, to prevent misunderstandings creeping in, you need as a matter of course to set out your pay expectations in your CV. You could, for example, do this by stating what you earn now and saying that this is a level you want to maintain or better. What you certainly want to avoid is being invited for an interview where the job would be twice the work for half the salary! Sadly, this happens more than you may think and the result is that everyone's time is wasted.

DISAPPOINTMENT AND DISCOURAGEMENT

Apart from timewasting, experiences like Jo's can have a more insidious effect. Attending a series of interviews, getting the job, and then finding the pay isn't up to scratch is disappointing, to say the least. Chalk up a few more experiences like this and you will find that your disappointment turns into discouragement. You will start to feel that there is nothing out there for you and this might cause you to do one of the following:

- lower your sights and tone down your ambitions
- give up altogether because you see what you're trying to do as a hopeless cause.

Needless to say, neither is good and one of the main benefits of making your aims clear in your CV is that you don't get into the situation where disappointment and discouragement take over.

COACH'S TIP

Quality, not quantity

The popular view that a CV is there to get you interviews leads to people judging their success in terms of the number of interviews they get. However, the interview count is meaningless if the jobs are not up to expectations. A far better measure of success is to look at how many of the interviews are for jobs that interest you and which you would take if they were offered to you.

There's more on ways of measuring the effectiveness of CVs later in the book.

PRESENTING THE REAL *YOU*

A CV should always aim to present you in a way that accurately reflects:

- who you **are**
- what you can **do**.

COACHING SESSION 11

Should a CV be 'economical with the truth'?

Here is another case study for you to consider:

Case study: John

After a flaming row in the office, John told his boss, Kate, what she could do with her job. He then added a few home truths about her management style – remarks that hit home and from which, John realized straight away, there would be no going back.

However, after the exhilarating thrill of putting Kate in her place had died down, the reality kicked in. For the first time in his life, John was a man without a job.

Later on, over a beer with one of his friends, John poured out his troubles. He needed another job and he needed one quickly before his funds ran out. The friend was sympathetic but at the same time pointed out that, with John's experience and qualifications, it wouldn't be too long before someone snapped him up. John was less sure. What, for example, did he put in his CV about his reason for leaving? A bust-up with the managing partner wasn't going to look good. The friend agreed but made the point that John could put in his CV that he'd been made redundant. After all, who was going to bother to check up? And even if they did, no one would think badly of John for glossing over the truth. Most other people in his position would do exactly the same.

1. What are your thoughts on the dilemma facing John? Does he tell the truth or does he do what his friend suggests?

   _____

   _____

   _____

2. Now put yourself into the shoes of an employer who is considering John for a key position. How would your views on him alter if you found out that the information he'd given in his CV was incorrect?

   _____

   _____

   _____

   _____

Everyone makes mistakes

All employers are different, so, while some would take a lenient view of having the wool pulled over their eyes, others (the majority perhaps) would see it as evidence of a flawed character – someone who is prepared to stoop to dishonesty, however minor, if it serves to further their own ends.

John may have made a mistake by losing his cool and giving Kate a piece of his mind. Yet, at the same time, everyone makes mistakes, and by and large people who own up to their mistakes are people you can do business with.

 COACH'S TIP

Honesty is the best policy

Employers don't expect people to be perfect but they do expect them to be honest.

COACHING SESSION 12

Should your CV ever exaggerate?

Imagine that you have seen a job advertised where one of the stipulations is experience that you don't have. The job is a good job and one you would dearly love to get, so it crosses your mind to design your CV in a way that makes it seem that you have had more experience than is really the case.

Apart from being found out, what dangers would you be exposing yourself to if you went ahead with this plan?

_____

_____

_____

_____

_____

_____

_____

_____

_____

Round pegs in round holes

Selection is about finding the right people, and employers will only be able to do this if they are given an accurate picture of what individuals are capable of doing. Presenting employers with an accurate picture is the job of your CV. If, by reading your CV, employers can see your qualifications and what experience you've had, they will be able to make a judgement about whether or not you're a suitable candidate for the job. Ensuring that employers get their judgements right is as much in your interest as it is in theirs. One of the worst-case scenarios for you as you seek to advance your career is finding yourself in a job where you're out of your depth. Employers are usually quick to act in these situations and the fallout for you could be catastrophic.

 COACH'S TIP

You and your prospective employer are allies

You don't want a job that is beyond your capabilities, just as employers don't want to hire people who are going to fail. Employers are on the same mission as you.

Use your CV to present a true picture

In your CV always aim to present a true picture of who you are and what you can do, then leave it to employers to decide whether you should be invited to an interview or not. For example, if there are shortfalls in your experience and/or qualifications, don't try to disguise the fact. Some employers will be happy to live with the shortfalls whereas others won't. In the latter instance, there is no point in letting the application proceed any further. The sooner it is stopped in its tracks, the better.

 NEXT STEPS

The job market is full of people who are thrashing round aimlessly and, as a consequence, not achieving much. One of the reasons for this aimlessness is their failure to transmit messages about themselves and their ambitions:

- to the market they're trying to access

- in terms that the market will understand.

It is rather like having a market stall where the goods you're selling are kept under wraps so no one can see them. The wrong customers are attracted and some of them won't have enough money to buy the goods, but who's to blame except you?

The message of this chapter is that you must make it clear to everyone what you want out of life and use your CV as the vehicle for this transparency. Make your CV work for you. Make it deliver what you want it to deliver and not something that disappoints you, wastes your time or lands you in deep water when jobs turn out not to be suitable for you.

You are now ready to start work on your CV by getting the structure into place and deciding what order you need to put information in. This is the subject of the next chapter.

TAKEAWAYS

Have you ever found yourself in an interview that was a complete waste of time? After reading this chapter, do you think your CV could have been to blame for not communicating your ambitions clearly enough? What do you plan to do in future to show the world where you are coming from and what you are seeking to achieve?

_____

_____

_____

_____

_____

_____

_____

_____

Do you have any skeletons in your cupboard? How did you deal with these skeletons when you last had the job of putting a CV together? As a result of reading this chapter, will you be doing anything differently in the future?

_____

_____

_____

_____

_____

_____

_____

_____

_____

_____

Did the section on using your CV to flag up your pay expectations make you think? Will you follow the advice?

_____

_____

_____

_____

_____

_____

_____

_____

_____

_____

In CVs that you have designed in the past, do you think you have been guilty of over-egging your experience in the hope that it will get you an interview? Do you now see the dangers? Make a note of what you think you have learned about the importance of accuracy in describing who you are and what you can do.

_____

_____

_____

_____

_____

_____

_____

_____

_____

_____

Is there anything you have read in this chapter that has caused you change your thinking about how to approach the job of designing a CV? What are the most important lessons you have learned?

_____

_____

_____

_____

_____

_____

_____

_____

_____

_____

3 GETTING THE STRUCTURE IN PLACE

OUTCOMES FROM THIS CHAPTER

- Know how to design the framework for your CV.
- Grasp the importance of a good first page.
- Know what to put in a CV and what to leave out.
- Understand the importance of contact information and of making sure it works.

COACHING SESSION 13

Revision tick list

Here is a tick list to go through that summarizes the main lessons in the book so far. Use it as a short revision exercise before you make a start on this chapter.

1. A good CV is an important part of making a good first impression. ☐
2. To work for you, a CV has to make it clear (a) where you're coming from and (b) what you're seeking to achieve. ☐
3. To stand up to the 'one quick read' test, a CV needs to be concise and relevant to whatever task you want it to perform. ☐
4. There has got to be enough interest in a CV for readers to feel they want to read it from start to finish. ☐

CREATING THE FRAMEWORK

When you need a CV, you usually find you need one straight away. You might see a great job advertised and you want to get off an application fast, or rumours might start flying round your office that a headcount cut is on the way, meaning that you need to get some irons in the fire as soon as you can. What will help you to react quickly to situations such as these is to have a framework around which you can design a CV that will perform the task you want it to perform.

What do you need?

You probably own (or have access to) a PC with a standard word-processing package already installed. A good-quality inkjet or laser printer is essential, so, if you don't have one and you want your CVs to look good, it may be a sensible investment.

COACHING SESSION 14

Make sure your word-processing software is up to date

To make sure that the word-processing software you're using is compatible with everyone else's, send a test email with a blank file attachment from your home PC either to a friend who works in an office or to your email address at work. Check whether the file attachment opens successfully.

Get set up

The point was made in Chapter 1 that the default settings that come with most standard word-processing packages are absolutely fine. Problems arise only when people start tampering with them – for example, reducing the size of margins in an effort to get more on the page. Don't do this. You will end up with something that isn't pleasing to the eye. In other words, it won't be employer-friendly.

Fonts and font sizes

Again, this point has been touched on already. Stick to conventional fonts and font sizes. Arial 11- or 12-point is fine. Times New Roman is equally acceptable. Don't be tempted to use fonts that fall outside the mainstream because you think they add interest or 'say something' about you. Adding interest is great, but it is best achieved by making sure that what goes into your CV is **relevant** to what you want it to do for you.

White space

White space is pleasing to the eye (employer-friendly), whereas a page of text that is crammed in with no line spaces between sections is the opposite. Be consistent with the number of line spaces you leave between sections and headings (two is fine).

Headings

Use bold or underlining to pick out headings, but not both.

Number and name your pages

Numbering the pages of your CV is a good idea. You may want to email it and, if you do, you will want to make sure that the person printing it out and assembling it at the other end will put the pages in the right order. CVs sent in the post may be stapled together but they may come apart, so the issue of putting the pages back together in the right order arises again. Simple though they sound, steps such as these ensure that your CV is read in the way you want it to be read.

Another tip is to put your name on every page. This will make sure your CV doesn't get mixed up with someone else's. Use a header or a footer for this purpose, so what you end up with is:

Polly Perfect – CV

Page 1 of 3

Saying 'Page 1 of 3' is a way of ensuring that pages aren't left out when the CV is run off from an email (this happens more often than you may think).

A GOOD FIRST PAGE

Remember the point about CVs not always being read from start to finish? What happens is that readers read so far then switch off because they have seen nothing that interests them.

COACHING SESSION 15

The all-important first page

The following example shows the first page of Polly Perfect's CV. Say in the space below (a) what you think is wrong with it and (b) how you think she could improve it.

(a)

_____

_____

_____

(b)

_____

_____

_____

Curriculum Vitae

Name: Polly Perfect

Address: 13, Sea View Close

                               Portchester on Sea

                               PC99 9XX

Email: pollyp@xxxxxxx

Phone: xxxx xxxxxx (home)

                               xxxx xxxxxx (mobile)

Driving Licence: Clean

Health: Good (non-smoker)

Education/Qualifications

1985–1991   Oakwood County Primary School

1991–1996   Watery Downs Comprehensive School

Examinations passed: GCSE English (1) Art (1), Geography (2)
German (3) Maths (4) Food Technology (4)

1996–1998   Portchester Sixth Form College

Examinations passed: GCE A level: Art (B) Media Studies (C)
Geography (C)

Why keep reading?

Polly Perfect is a fictitious applicant for a middle-management position with a large chain of electrical goods retailers. The first page of her CV provides information on where she lives and how to contact her if the reader should decide to take her application any further. She has no health problems, she doesn't smoke and she drives her car carefully. At school, it appears she was good at art, then she went on to do three A levels – but so what? Who is really interested in half this information and, more to the point, what relevance does it have to the job for which she is applying? What is there that draws the reader's interest and makes them feel they want to turn over and look at the next page? The short answer is *nothing*.

Why a good front page is important

Apart from your cover letter, the front page of your CV is what the reader sees first. It is important therefore that what hits them in the eye is enough about you for them to take a positive view of your suitability for the job – enough to encourage them to want to find out more.

The need for a good front page is greatest when you are designing a CV for attacking the visible job market – when you are applying for jobs that have been advertised and where your CV has to be capable of making you stand out from all the other applications that the employer will have received. It is just as important when you are sending out unsolicited CVs to employers – you need to stand out from the crowd.

What are your strong points?

Your strong points are your **key matches** – where there is a match between what you have to offer and the qualities that the reader of your CV is seeking. It is your strong points that need to feature on your front page.

 COACH'S TIP

Include your key matches on the front page

This matching of attributes is important and ensures that anything you put in a CV is relevant to the task you want it to perform. If the employer is looking for someone who can conduct a business meeting in fluent German and you have this skill, then this is a key match. You may be equally fluent in Russian, but if the employer has no need for a Russian speaker then you are looking at information that has general interest only and, while it may be worth a mention somewhere in your CV, it is not front-page material.

There will be more on matching skills and achievements to the task you want your CV to perform as you work your way through the book.

How your front page will look

In the framework version of your CV, your front page will consist of your personal information, information on how to contact you and a section headed 'Key skills and achievements'. This last section will be blank because what goes here (your list of key matches) will be different every time you put together a CV.

WHAT TO INCLUDE IN YOUR CV

Remember, at this point you are putting together a framework rather than a finished version, so 'what to put in' will consist of information that isn't going to change from one CV to the next.

You will need to consider things like your name - which may be more complicated that you might think - and other personal and contact information, and whether or not to include a photograph of yourself. You will also need to include your employment history and give details of your education and training.

Photographs

♟♟ COACHING SESSION 16

Photograph or no photograph?

Do you have any views on putting a photograph of yourself on the front page of your CV? Explain why you think it's a good or bad idea.

_____

_____

_____

_____

_____

_____

_____

_____

_____

Will a picture of your smiling face on the front page of your CV make a good first impression when it lands on someone's desk? Or will it have the opposite effect?

It should be said straight away that there are widely differing opinions on the value of putting a photograph on the front page of your CV. If the job calls for someone who is photogenic, then, fair enough, it's a way of saying that you are. If, on the other hand, it's an ordinary run-of-the-mill job, there are arguments in favour and arguments against. Selection is a subjective business and, it has to be said, someone not liking the way you look in a photograph could put paid to your chances of getting on the interview list.

If you do decide to put a photograph on the front page of your CV, go through the following checklist first:

- The camera doesn't lie and the typical head-and-shoulders shots that people put on their CVs are not always very flattering. As a safeguard, get a second opinion on your photograph from someone you trust and whom you can rely on to be honest with you.

- Make sure your hair is tidy. If your hair's untidy, (a) readers of your CV will notice and (b) it will have them wondering what the rest of you looks like.

- Smiles are not engaging if they look forced or false. Worse still, they could send out a subliminal message that you're not a person to be trusted.

- Make sure that what you're wearing (or what can be seen of it) is consistent with the attire you would normally wear for work. A photograph taken on holiday or on a night out with your friends is probably not going to do you much good on the first impressions front.

- It may be worth investing in having your photograph taken by a professional photographer who will not only have the right equipment but will also be able to advise you on how to pose and present yourself.

If reading this list has served to put you off, then perhaps it's best to forget the idea. A CV without a photograph is fine.

 COACH'S TIP

Project the right image

When choosing a photo for your CV, the main question to ask yourself is whether it projects the image you want it to project. Does it send the right message?

What's in a name?

Staying with the front page of your CV, the first item at the top will be your name.

◎◎ COACHING SESSION 17

How should you style yourself?

There are many ways in which you could style your name on your CV:

- Steven James Smith
- Steven Smith
- Steve Smith
- Steven Smith (Mr)
- Steve Smith MSc CEng

In your opinion, which of these sounds better, and why?

_____

_____

_____

_____

_____

_____

Consider the following:

- **First names** Use the first name by which you are normally known to your work colleagues. In the exercise Steve is fine if that's what people call him.

- **Titles** Titles such as Mr, Mrs, Ms or Miss are best avoided in a CV because they can make you sound old-fashioned and/or standoffish (neither is good).

- **Letters after your name** Use any letters after your name that are relevant to the position for which you are applying because they act as a quick way of telling your readers that you're qualified. On the other hand, don't use letters after your name if they have no relevance. It can look pretentious, especially to someone who doesn't have the same qualifications.

How to contact you

Contact information is important, so it should feature on the front page of your CV immediately after your name. Contact information should include:

- your full postal address
- your private email address (except in the case of a CV you are designing for business purposes)
- your home phone number
- your mobile number.

In some cases, you will be able to include the number on which you can be contacted at work. For example, if you're at risk of redundancy it will be no secret that you're looking for another job and your employer will probably be doing all they can to help you. However, if this is not the case and if the last thing you want is your bosses finding out that you're thinking of moving on, then having to take a call in the middle of the office from a prospective employer could be embarrassing.

COACH'S TIP

Make sure you're contactable

What's important about listing all your points of contact is that there is more than one way of getting in touch with you. If, for example, an employer tries ringing you at home on your landline and the call isn't answered or the number is engaged, then there is a fall-back in the shape of your mobile or the option of sending you an email.

Later in this chapter there will be more on checking that the points of contact you have given in your CV work when they are put to the test. Making sure that recipients of your CV can get hold of you if they need to is important when you consider that the general idea of a CV is to encourage them to want to take things a stage further.

Date of birth

In years gone by it was normal to put your date of birth on the front page of your CV. Now attitudes have changed, with the result that some candidates include their dates of birth and some don't. Which is correct?

COACHING SESSION 18

Date of birth or no date of birth?

What are your views on putting your date of birth on the front page of your CV? Say what you would do and use the space below to explain why.

_____

_____

_____

_____

_____

_____

_____

In these enlightened times, age is no longer supposed to be a factor when assessing someone's suitability for a role. However, you also need to consider that in recent years employers have increasingly become the targets for litigation, including litigation from unsuccessful job applicants claiming that they have been the victims of unlawful discrimination, including discrimination on grounds of age. The result is that many employers now take the view that, at the selection stage, they prefer not to know an applicant's age because, if they don't, they can hardly be accused of discrimination.

Though the debate goes on, it is probably true to say that most authorities today would advise you to leave your date of birth _off_ your CV. The point could be made, of course, that other information in someone's CV (for example, the dates when they attended school) gives a good indication of their age.

Medical history

There is much the same kind of debate about applicants giving details of their medical history in their CVs. The issue here is disability discrimination. If you declare a medical condition, it could fall under the heading of a disability, so employers may feel they would rather not have this information.

Smoking information

If you are a non-smoker, what about making the point in your CV? Will it do you any favours?

◯◯ COACHING SESSION 19

Is it worth mentioning that you're a non-smoker?

Do you have any views on this? Why would an employer be drawn to a non-smoker?

Write your answers here.

_____

_____

_____

_____

_____

_____

Many employers don't like smokers. There are several reasons for this, the main ones being the following:

- Smokers tend to be less healthy, which means, to an employer's way of thinking, that they may be more likely to take time off work.

- The need to have cigarette breaks causes work to be disrupted.

- The gaggle of smokers standing outside the front door of many employers' premises gives a bad impression to visitors.

- In warm weather, the smell of smoke drifting in from outside through open windows can be disagreeable.

- Disciplinary issues can arise from breaches of employers' smoking policies. (Employers don't want to spend their time dealing with disciplinary issues.)

All of the above underline why it's worth mentioning in your CV that you're a non-smoker.

Your employment history

List your jobs in reverse order, starting with the present or most recent one first and working your way backwards. Why? Because what you're doing now (or what you did last) will be more interesting to your readers than what you did at the start of your career. The description of what you did (or do) in the jobs you have held should be left blank in the framework version of your CV because what you say needs to be relevant to the task you want your CV to perform. If, for example, you want a CV so that you can apply for a job where one of the requirements is experience in using a certain technique, then you will need to bring this out in your employment history at the expense of information that isn't relevant.

 COACH'S TIP

Keep it relevant

Bear in mind, when creating your framework employment history, that you will need to amend it each time you prepare to send it out, to make it relevant to the particular job for which you are applying.

Your reasons for leaving jobs

Reasons for leaving jobs interest employers because they give insights into:

- what drives you
- how much you will put up with
- whether you've failed in any of the jobs (an indication that you could fail again).

○○ COACHING SESSION 20

Typical reasons for leaving a job found on CVs

Here are six reasons for leaving jobs taken from candidates' CVs. Say in each case:

- what is wrong with the reason the candidate has given
- how you would better it.

1. 'Poor pay'

_____

_____

_____

2. 'Broken promises'

_____

_____

_____

3. 'Too much travelling'

_____

_____

_____

4. 'No training opportunities'

_____

_____

_____

5. 'CEO's attitude to management staff'

_____

_____

_____

6. 'Redundancy'

_____

_____

_____

In giving your reasons, try to turn a negative into the positive. This subject was touched on earlier in the book in the context of describing your ambitions. As a breed, employers don't warm to people who grumble because they see them as potential troublemakers and not the kind of people they want on their team. Reasons for leaving 1–5 are essentially grumbles and that is the problem with them. They create an unfortunate impression and, when there is nothing to balance it up, the unfortunate impression has a tendency to stick (back to the reverse halo effect and the importance of first impressions).

 COACH'S TIP

Stress the positives

Always frame your reasons for leaving jobs in a positive way by focusing attention on what you sought to gain from making the move rather than what you saw as the problems with the job you left. For example: 'To move to an organization where my skills would be better rewarded' sounds better than 'poor pay', even though it means much the same.

What's wrong with giving redundancy as the reason why you left a job? Isn't it a reason why a lot of people lose their jobs? Isn't it a way of saying that it wasn't your fault?

Increasingly these days, employers want to go behind the reasons for redundancy. Why?

- Some people use the term 'redundancy' to describe any loss of job. For example, someone saying they have been made redundant could be someone who has been sacked for misconduct.

- In some organizations, the criteria for selecting people for redundancy include items such as attendance or job performance.

When you give redundancy as the reason why you left a job, it is a good idea to add a few words to allay employers' fears – for example, writing 'redundancy following the closure of the company's UK operation' makes it clear that losing your job was not your fault.

Education

For the same reason as you did for your employment history, list the educational institutions you have attended in reverse order: the ones you attended most recently are probably going to have most relevance to the task you want your CV to perform. They could, for example, include the institutions where you studied for your vocational qualifications. List in each case the dates (from and to) when you attended and details of any relevant qualifications. Identify any current courses of study together with the envisaged completion dates.

Training courses

List any relevant training courses you have attended together with the dates and the names of the course organizers/institutions.

Languages/information technology (IT) skills

Include these where the information is relevant to the career you are in (or the ambition you want to pursue).

Ambitions

Leave this section blank in the framework version of your CV. It is important to match your ambitions to what the recipient of your CV will be seeking to see.

Salary

The point has been made already that, even though you may not be designing the CV to get you a better-paid job, it is still important to make it clear what you're earning now and what future level of salary would be acceptable to you. Where your package includes significant perks (e.g. company car, medical plan, share options, etc.), this also needs to be made clear.

Personal statement

With some of the tasks you want your CV to perform, it may help to include a personal statement. For example, if you want to use your CV to cut your working time down from five to three days a week, you could explain why by making a statement in your CV. Without this information, employers picking up your CV may be left to draw their own conclusions (never a good idea). Even worse, they may think you've made a mistake and applied for the wrong job.

Period of notice

Prospective employers with vacant positions to fill will want to know how quickly you can start if they decide to offer you the job. Your period of notice is therefore something you need to put in your CV. Your period of notice is whatever it says in your terms and conditions of employment.

COACHING SESSION 21

What should Ramesh do?

Here is a case study for you to consider:

Case study: Ramesh

Ramesh is desperate to find another job. Two months ago a new CEO arrived on the scene – a woman who is poles apart from Ramesh in the way she feels the business should be run. There have already been clashes and Ramesh can see that his days are numbered, hence the need for him to prepare a new CV. However, while Ramesh is confident that his know-how and experience will interest other employers, he is worried that his six-month period of notice will put many of them off.

What would you do in Ramesh's position? Give your answer here.

_____

_____

_____

_____

_____

_____

_____

_____

_____

One of the reasons employers put key people on long periods of notice is to make it difficult for them if it ever crossed their minds to take their talents elsewhere. So Ramesh's fears are well founded. Six months is a long time to hold a vacant slot open and many employers would be put off, especially when other candidates are available who could be on board in a matter of weeks.

However, what usually happens with these long periods of notice is that they become the focal point for negotiation. Using Ramesh as the example, if he and his new boss are not seeing eye to eye, there could be common ground when it came to agreeing a date on which he could be released. In any case, the likelihood of an employer holding someone who wants to leave to a six- or twelve-month period of notice is remote in the extreme.

When considering what he should put in his CV, Ramesh must face the issue of his notice period. While the fact that his employment is subject to six months' notice is inescapable, something that would soften the blow as far as prospective employers are concerned would be to add a few words along the lines of 'negotiable in the event of a suitable position being offered to me'.

By and large, employers only put key people on long periods of notice so, if you are subject to one, it's a sign that your organization places a high value on you. What this means is that it can also play to your advantage.

COACH'S TIP

Warning!

People put in Ramesh's position are often drawn into making statements like 'My employment is subject to six months' notice, but I would be prepared to give less.' People prepared to take their contractual obligations lightly do not impress prospective employers.

Unemployed

If you are unemployed, make a point of mentioning it in your CV (the employment history section is a good place). There are few advantages to being unemployed, but one of them is that you can start another job immediately. You may find that this hits the spot with an employer who is in a hurry to get a vacancy filled.

Nationality

British, Norwegian, Australian – put your nationality in your CV. Where it is relevant, include information on residential status and work permits, etc. Employers need to know that they wouldn't be breaking the law if they decided to offer you a job.

Leisure activities

Don't fill up half a page of your CV with information on what you do in your spare time. In a world where employers expect a high level of commitment from their staff, long lists of pastimes can leave them wondering how you manage to fit work in. Listing sports where you could be injured is another mistake. Injuries mean having to have time off work. Strange hobbies are best not mentioned. Strange hobbies tend to be the preserve of strange people.

References

Give the names, addresses and daytime telephone numbers of two referees. Ideally, one of your referees will be able to vouch for the quality of your work – for example, a former boss. The other should be someone who knows you personally and who will be able to vouch for your character.

COACH'S TIP

Get your referee's permission

Don't put the name of a referee in your CV unless you have spoken to them and got their permission first.

TESTING YOUR CONTACT INFORMATION AND MAKING SURE IT WORKS

Make sure your contact information is working well before you have a need to send your CV to anyone (though not too long before, obviously). The aim is to ensure that someone trying to get hold of you using the contact information you have given will be able to do so without difficulty.

This is important because, once your CV goes out, there is every possibility that someone picking it up and reading it will want to speak to you. Perhaps it will be because they want to resolve some minor query but it may be to invite you to an interview. What you don't want at this stage, therefore, is for callers to find that they run into a brick wall because:

- the phone numbers you've given either aren't answered or are constantly engaged
- the voicemail messages they leave aren't returned
- there is no reply to the emails and/or text messages they send you.

The amount of gadgetry on the market has mushroomed in recent years, so today there is no excuse for being hard to contact. Making it easy for people who want to get hold of you is all part of being 'employer-friendly'. The next coaching session will test whether you are, without knowing it, putting barriers in the way of people who may be trying to contact you. Aim for as many ticks in the boxes as possible.

⚉⚉ COACHING SESSION 22

Make sure you're contactable

What would happen if someone wanted to speak to you about an interview and phoned you at home at 7 p.m. tonight?

1. Would you be in? ☐
2. Would anyone be in? ☐
3. If the number is engaged, is there an answerphone message? ☐

Now ask yourself the following questions:

1. Would a caller who couldn't get through be able to leave a message on voicemail? ☐
2. Would you know within an hour that someone had left a message on voicemail? ☐
3. Are you diligent about checking voicemail messages on your home phone? ☐
4. What if you're not there? Does anyone else check the messages? ☐

With regard to your mobile phone:

1. Is it with you all the time? ☐
2. Is it always switched on? ☐
3. Are you diligent about checking voicemail messages and missed calls? ☐
4. Do you respond quickly to text messages? ☐

Finally, consider your personal email address:

1. Do you check your messages often? ☐
2. Are you kitted out to access messages when you are not at home? ☐
3. Do you respond quickly to emails that are sent to you? ☐

Carrying out an exercise such as this is designed to throw up some points for action such as:

*   After sending out a CV, do you need to introduce some discipline at home about how long people spend on the phone?
*   With regard to your home phone, do you need a facility to divert calls to your mobile?
*   Alternatively, do you need a facility on your mobile that alerts you when callers have left a voicemail message on your home phone?
*   Do you need to be more disciplined about checking messages and missed calls?
*   If you're on the move a lot, do you need a way of checking your email messages (e.g. a smartphone)?

COACH'S TIP

Warning!

Employers in the shape of busy managers will try only for so long with people who are hard to contact before giving up and moving on to someone else. All the effort you put into preparing your CV will then be completely wasted.

COACHING SESSION 23

Sample framework CV

On the following pages is an example of a framework CV.

Pick out what you consider to be good or bad in the example and give your reasons.

Curriculum Vitae

Name   Jane Excellent

Address   Flat 4
Quayside House
River Street
PORTCHESTER-ON-SEA
PC2 1AA

Email   janee@xxx.com

Telephone   Home: xxxxx xxxxxx (after 6 p.m. – except Thursday)
Office: xxxxx xxxxxx
Mobile: xxxxx xxxxxx

Key skills/achievements

Education

1981–1987	City Comprehensive School
1987–1990	Queens' Commercial College (part-time day release)
2000–2005	Portchester College of Further Education (evenings)

Qualifications

O levels: English Language (B), Business Studies (B), Geography (C), Art (D) 1987

RSA Typewriting: Stages 1, 2 and 3 (1987–1990)

RSA English Language: Stages 1, 2 and 3 (1987–1990)

Pitman Shorthand: 90 and 100 wpm (1988–1990)

RSA Word Processing: Stages 1, 2 and 3 (1999–2000)

RSA Teachers' Diploma in Administration Skills (2002)

D32/33 Assessors' Awards (2002)

RSA/OCR Integrated Business Technology Stage 3 (2005)

IT skills

I am fully conversant with all versions of Microsoft Word, Excel, Access, PowerPoint and Publisher.

I act as IT trouble-shooter in my present company. I am responsible for purchasing all hardware and software.

Ambitions

Salary

I currently earn £30k per annum. I am seeking a salary of £35k minimum.

Employment history

1995– present   Portchester Building Supplies Limited

Position held: Secretary/PA to Managing Director. In addition to secretarial duties I am responsible for payroll and IT in a company with an annual turnover of £5 million.

1988–1994   Martin & Associates

Position held: Administration Assistant in small firm of solicitors. Telephone calls, correspondence, word processing letters, legal documents etc. using Microsoft Word (initially self-taught). Reason for leaving: to pursue ambition to become a Secretary/PA.

1987–1988   Furnival and Sons Limited

12 months' placement with firm of paper merchants. General office duties: typing, filing, inputting data etc. Reason for leaving: end of placement.

Period of notice

One month

Nationality

British

Health

Good (non-smoker)

Leisure-time activities

Swimming. Going to the theatre. Keeping fit – I visit the gym twice a week.

References

Work: Graham Martin, Senior partner, Martin & Associates (Tel: xxxx xxxx)

Personal: June Griffiths, Senior Lecturer in Computer Studies, Porchester College of Further Education (Tel: xxxx xxxx)

NEXT STEPS

One of the many challenges of living in a fast-moving world is the need to respond to opportunities quickly. Having a framework CV in place (the subject of this chapter) means not having to start from scratch should the need for a CV arise urgently. You can concentrate on the fine-tuning rather than find you're spending time digging in the backs of drawers for old certificates or looking for information that will tell you when you started in a job you left 15 years ago. While it is important that you custom-build every CV you produce, a lot of information won't change from one CV to the next (such as your personal details and details of your education and training).

CVs are there to perform the task you want them to perform, and in today's difficult world one of the tasks a CV is most commonly called upon to perform is to attack job markets that are competitively fought over. The challenge is therefore one of designing a CV that will engage with and overcome the competition. This is the subject of the next chapter.

Do you already have a framework version of your CV stored in a form that you can edit and work on? If not, do you think that designing a framework CV would be a worthwhile exercise to carry out? Target a date for having your framework CV in place.

_____

_____

_____

_____

_____

_____

_____

_____

_____

_____

Did you learn anything useful from reading the section on creating the framework? Is there anything you hadn't thought to do previously? Make a note of any points here.

_____

_____

_____

_____

_____

_____

_____

_____

_____

_____

Did the message about having a good first page cause you to think? Will you be changing your first page as a result?

_____

_____

_____

_____

_____

_____

_____

_____

_____

_____

_____

Are you satisfied that the contact information in your CV works and that someone trying to get hold of you would be able to do so without experiencing any difficulties? Make a note of anything you plan to do to make life easier for people who want to talk to you.

_____

_____

_____

_____

_____

_____

_____

_____

_____

_____

As a result of reading this chapter, will you be inserting any information in your CVs that wasn't there previously?

_____

_____

_____

_____

_____

_____

_____

_____

_____

_____

_____

_____

Conversely, will you be leaving anything out? Say why you feel the information is no longer relevant.

_____

_____

_____

_____

_____

_____

_____

_____

_____

_____

_____

_____

4 ATTACKING THE COMPETITION

✔ OUTCOMES FROM THIS CHAPTER

- Know how to design a CV for cracking tough job markets.
- Know how to address the challenge of overcoming the competition.
- Consider how to make your CV stand out from the rest.
- Understand what it takes to make it on to the interview list.

CRACKING TOUGH JOB MARKETS

Everyone knows that good jobs that have been advertised widely attract applicants in large numbers. Sometimes employers are prepared for the avalanche but often they're taken by surprise. However, prepared or not, the first task they face is going though the pile of applications they've received and picking out the applicants who sound like they're worth asking along for an interview.

⚲⚲ COACHING SESSION 24

Possible criteria for choosing interviewees

Do you have any experience of drawing up an interview list? How did you proceed and what criteria did you use for deciding which candidates to call in and which to turn down? Write your answer here.

_____

_____

_____

_____

How interview lists are decided

Managers tasked with going though a large number of job applications usually have to fit this in with everything else that demands their attention. This has the following results:

- The more applications there are, the less time will be given to reading each one.
- 'Reading' often consists of no more than a quick flick-through.
- Readers' eyes will be focused on picking out points of interest (points of interest to *them*).
- CVs are not always read from start to finish (a point touched on earlier in this book).
- CVs are rarely read twice (once in the turn-down pile, they tend to stay there).

What this means is that, in competitive job situations, what you have to offer has got to:

- come across in one quick read because it won't get another chance
- match up with what the employer wants and this, too, has to come across first time.

The importance of your cover letter

When you submit a job application, what you normally do is send in your CV with a cover letter attached to it. What the employer reads therefore is not just your CV but your cover letter also – in fact, your cover letter is what the employer usually sees first. For this reason, cover letters are just as important as CVs, and this is especially the case when you're up against tough competition.

The importance of presentation

When there are dozens of other applicants for the job, any CV that comes in that is untidy and/or riddled with poor grammar and spelling mistakes will tend to be binned automatically. Sadly, it's the poor grammar and spelling mistakes that catch the reader's eye, not the applicant's good points.

Also under the heading of CVs that are binned automatically are those that don't follow any logical order – typically where the information in them is jumbled up in a way that may have made sense to their creators but doesn't to anyone else.

WHAT EMPLOYERS ARE LOOKING FOR

It's worth saying again: what one employer will see as a key attribute for a job, another employer won't see in the same way – emphasizing once more why it's important to tailor your CV to the requirements of the job for which you're applying.

COACHING SESSION 25

Finding out what an employer wants

How would you set about determining what an employer sees as the key attributes for a job you've seen advertised? Where would you look for clues?

Give your answer in bullet-point form.

_____

_____

_____

_____

_____

_____

_____

_____

_____

_____

_____

_____

_____

_____

_____

_____

_____

_____

_____

_____

_____

_____

Read the ad for the job

The job ad itself is an obvious place to look for insights into what the employer sees as important qualities. 'The ideal candidate will have ...' 'This position calls for someone with ...' Here, employers are telling you exactly what they want. However, the ad may also tell you how you can access a full job description or a person specification – for example, by visiting the employer's website. Where information such as this is made available to you, make sure you access it and read it carefully.

Search the Internet

This is a quick and easy way of getting background information on an employer, including insights into the way they see themselves. For example, you may learn from an employer's website that they take a strong ethical stance on promoting Third World agriculture, so the marathon you ran to raise money for a famine relief charity last year may have more relevance to your application than you thought. You could include it as one of your reasons for applying for the job.

Tap into your networks

There may be someone in your circle of professional contacts who can give you some inside information on what the employer tends to look for when it comes to hiring people – information you may not be able to get from any other source. Often, it's a case of just asking around – this is especially the case in tightly knit professions where everyone tends to know everyone else.

Inspired guesswork

There is nothing wrong with inspired guesswork, especially when information would otherwise be thin on the ground. Here it is often a case of assembling a few facts about an organization and then putting two and two together. For example: in an industry that is highly competitive it's a safe bet that there will be a high level of interest in anyone who is working for a rival business – or who has worked for a rival business in the past.

ENGAGING THE COMPETITION

Where there is a lot of interest in a job, you will need to have some way of making your application stand out from the others. The following coaching session will invite you to reflect on how you might do this.

🗣🗣 COACHING SESSION 26

How would you make your CV stand out?

Based on what you have learned so far, what are your thoughts on how to make your CV one of the ones an employer picks out? What would you do to give yourself the best chance you can of being put on the interview list?

_____

_____

_____

_____

_____

Key matches/strong points

What catches employers' eyes is information in a CV that they are going to find **relevant** to the position that they are hoping to fill. This is where you go back to picking out where there are matches between the following:

- What you have to offer
- What attributes the employer is looking for

You will recall that in the previous chapter these were referred to as your **key matches** (you will also see them referred to as **strong points**). It is your strong points that readers of your CV will focus on, and what happens from there depends to a large extent on how strong your strong points are compared with what other candidates have to offer.

Your strong points could include any of the following:

- You hold the right qualifications.
- You have the right kind of experience.
- You have been given the right kind of training.
- You have some other attribute or quality relevant to the position for which you are applying – for example, you live in the right place, so the employer wouldn't have the trouble and expense of having to relocate you.

! COACH'S TIP

Relevance, above all

You may have many other outstanding qualities, but if they're not relevant to the position for which you're applying, they won't tip the balance when it comes to deciding whether or not to put you on the interview list.

COACHING SESSION 27

How did you make your last CV stand out?

Go back to the last job you applied for and list in bullet-point form what you saw at the time as your strong points – that is, what the employer concerned would see as the most compelling reasons for including you on the interview list.

_____

_____

_____

_____

_____

_____

_____

Now count up your bullet points. Are there more than six? If there are, go through the list again because you're probably including points that:

- aren't really strong points

- had little impact on your application

- would be better taken out in case they detract from what will make the difference in terms of setting you apart from other candidates.

When carrying out this exercise, remember that:

- you're up against competition

- some of the competition will be every bit as good as you are

- the reader may have looked at dozens of CVs before yours.

Bringing your strong points into prominence

Having a great set of strong points is all well and good, but they won't do much for you if they're buried somewhere in the deeper recesses of your CV where it will take a more detailed read than your CV is going to get to bring them into prominence. What you need therefore is to display your strong points in places where they can't fail to attract the reader's eye.

So where would you choose?

The two places that commend themselves most are:

1. on the **front page** of your CV (in the key skills/achievements section that you left blank when you prepared the framework version)

2. in your **cover letter** (the subject of cover letters is dealt with separately in Chapter 10).

Keep your strong points concise

Describing a strong point is a one- or two-sentence job. Otherwise, what you're trying to describe:

- will fail the 'one quick read' test
- won't fit on the front page of your CV when listed with your other strong points, and will therefore defeat the object.

 COACH'S TIP

Plain and simple

When describing strong points, stick to plain statements of fact. Don't, under any circumstances, descend into the kind of toe-curling self-eulogies that cut no ice at all with employers. Self-praise is no praise.

Back up your strong points

In the detail of your CV, you need to back up what you have said about yourself in your cover letter and in the key skills/achievements section on your front page. If, for example, you are claiming to have had experience of using a technique, and if this experience is a requirement of the job for which you are applying, then when you get to the employment history section of your CV you will need to show where on your path in life you have had the experience. This may mean that you afford more space in your employment history to this part of your career and do so at the expense of other (less relevant) information elsewhere.

COACH'S TIP

Strong points vs. conciseness

Giving your strong points prominence still needs to be consistent with keeping your CV concise and a quick and easy read. To achieve this, you may have to take out some cherished piece of information to make the necessary space. Console yourself with the fact that the strong point will have more bearing on whether you are picked for an interview or not.

Use their words

This is important. In their advertisements and job descriptions employers sometimes use words that you would not have chosen yourself – that is, their jargon is different from yours. In these situations, put your own preferences to one side and use their words so that there is no room for misunderstandings.

To save the bother of having to trawl through large numbers of applications, some employers have resorted to scanning CVs by computer. The software they use is programmed to pick up key words and phrases – so this is the process of searching for matches between the requirements of the job and what candidates have to offer, done in reverse. What this emphasizes is the importance of using the same terminology that the employer uses (terminology that the software will recognize).

🗩🗩 COACHING SESSION 28

Give some advice

Here is a short case study for you to consider:

Case study: Mike

Mike works for a large freight-handling business and he has seen a job advertised with one of his firm's leading competitors. Mike has been feeling for some time that he is stagnating and the job with the competitor would offer him the chance to step up the ladder as well as to earn a better salary with an attractive package of fringe benefits. However, what Mike realizes is that, if he applies for the job, he won't be the only one – indeed, word is already going round the office that several of his colleagues are also interested. Mike thinks hard. What, he wonders, can he do to make sure he is at the front of the queue? Then he hits on an idea. The advertisement asks for applicants to send their CVs in the post to the company's HR Manager, but what if he were to email his CV instead? Won't that guarantee it will get read before anyone else's? Won't that, in turn, boost his chances of getting an interview?

What do you think to Mike's idea? What advice would you give him?

_____

_____

_____

_____

_____

_____

_____

_____

_____

_____

_____

_____

_____

_____

Follow the instructions

Mike is not alone in seeing some advantage in deviating from the instructions that employers give in their advertisements. They wouldn't do this, though, if they knew how many CVs submitted in ways other than the correct one end up in the wrong place. For example, by emailing his CV rather than posting it, Mike could find that no one bothers to print it off or treats it as spam. The moral to this story is always do what the advertisement tells you to do and don't substitute your own ideas about 'what's best'.

COACH'S TIP

Warning!

Feeling that they're getting in before the rush and giving themselves an advantage, some applicants adopt the practice of delivering their CVs in person. They would not do this if they knew how many CVs have turned up months later stuffed in the back of the receptionist's drawer!

Don't delay

At the same time, don't hang about when you're sending in an application for a job that's been advertised. Employers will wait only so long and, when they sense that the flow of applications coming in is drying up, they will want to move on swiftly to the job of setting up interviews. Any CVs arriving after the interview list has been drawn up stand a good chance of not being read.

COACH'S TIP

Act quickly

Employers won't wait for you to put the finishing touches to your CV. One of the main reasons for having a framework in place is to give you the capacity to act quickly when opportunities present themselves.

🗩🗩 COACHING SESSION 29

Jane Excellent sends out her CV as part of a job application

Below is another CV for you to consider. In this example, Jane Excellent (whose framework CV appears in Chapter 2) is applying for the position of Secretary/PA to the CEO of a large financial institution headquartered in the city where she lives. The advertisement for the position mentions the need for someone with an up-to-date set of secretarial skills and a high level of shorthand proficiency. Jane has found out from her research that the firm has offices all over the world and, because of the nature of the job, she has guessed that it will entail handling sensitive information.

As before, pick out what you see as the good points in Jane's CV. Also say how you think she could improve it, bearing in mind that the position was given prominent block advertising in the local broadsheet.

Good points

_____

_____

_____

_____

_____

_____

_____

How it could be bettered

_____

_____

_____

_____

_____

_____

Curriculum Vitae

Name   Jane Excellent

Address   Flat 4

Quayside House

River Street

PORTCHESTER-ON-SEA

PC2 1AA

Email   janee@xxx.com

Telephone   home xxxxx xxxxxx (after 6 p.m. – except Thursday)

office xxxxx xxxxxx

mobile xxxxx xxxxxx

Key skills/achievements

- I have worked in a senior position as a secretary/PA for the last ten years.
- I am conversant with all versions of Microsoft Word. I currently use Word 2007
- My shorthand skills are proficient up to 100 wpm
- I am fully flexible. My working day knows no boundaries. I have no ties and I am used to working long and unsociable hours.
- I hold a full clean driving licence
- I am used to having access to highly confidential information. I am currently responsible for salaries and service contracts of senior staff. I attend board meetings and take minutes.
- I strive to keep my skills up to date by attending courses in my own time.

Education

1981–1987	City Comprehensive School
1987–1990	Queens' Commercial College (part-time day release)
2000–2005	Portchester College of Further Education (evenings)

Qualifications

GCE O level: English Language (B), Business Studies (B), Geography (C) Art (D) 1987

RSA Typewriting: Stages 1, 2 and 3 (1987–1990)

RSA English Language: Stages 1, 2 and 3 (1987–1990)

Pitman Shorthand: 90 and 100 wpm (1988–1990)

RSA Word Processing: Stages 1, 2 and 3 (1999–2000)

RSA Teachers' Diploma in Administration Skills (2002)

D32/33 Assessors' Awards (2002)

RSA/OCR Integrated Business Technology Stage 3 (2005)

IT skills

I am fully conversant with all versions of Microsoft Word, Excel, Access, PowerPoint and Publisher.

Ambitions

I am seeking a position as a Secretary/PA in a larger organization where I will be working with a wider cross-section of people.

Salary

I currently earn £30k per annum. I am seeking a salary of £35k minimum.

Nationality

British

Employment history

1995–present   Portchester Building Supplies Limited

Position held: Secretary/PA to Managing Director. In addition to secretarial duties I have responsibility for payroll and IT.

1988–1994   Martin & Associates

Position held: Administration Assistant in a small firm of solicitors. Telephone calls, correspondence, word processing letters, legal documents etc. using Microsoft Word (initially self-taught). Reason for leaving: to pursue ambition to become a Secretary/PA.

1987–1988   Furnival and Sons Limited

12 months' placement with firm of paper merchants. General office duties: typing, filing, inputting data etc. Reason for leaving: end of placement.

Period of notice

One month

Health

Good (non-smoker)

Leisure-time activities

Swimming. Going to the theatre. Keeping fit – I visit the gym twice a week.

References

Work: Graham Martin, Senior partner, Martin & Associates (Tel: xxxx xxxx)

Personal: June Griffiths, Senior Lecturer in Computer Studies, Portchester College of Further Education (Tel: xxxx xxxx)

 **NEXT STEPS**

This chapter has been about designing a CV to attack the advertised or visible job market, where the task is one of engaging with – and overcoming – competition. Here you have seen how employers faced with a surfeit of good candidates pick out those who put what they have to offer on display in a quick- and easy-to-read way. This contrasts with candidates who may be every bit as well qualified but whose attributes are buried in the detail of their CVs, so that an employer flicking through may not notice them. They end up on the reject pile, and when they get the letter advising them that they haven't been selected to attend an interview, they rack their brains wondering why. The answer, sadly, is that their CV didn't do the job it was supposed to do. It let them down.

So much for the visible job market, but what about its invisible counterpart – the jobs that aren't advertised for one reason or another and that are rumoured to be the best jobs? The next chapter looks at designing a CV for a mailshot, which is one of the ways of accessing opportunities that would otherwise be hidden from you. As you will find out, the challenges are very different.

TAKEAWAYS

Are you satisfied that CVs you've put together in the past would stand out? Is there anything you have learned from reading this chapter?

_____

_____

_____

_____

_____

_____

_____

_____

_____

Has reading this chapter caused you to have any further thoughts on what needs to go on your first page? What will you do in future that you haven't done in the past?

_____

_____

_____

_____

_____

_____

_____

_____

_____

_____

_____

As a result of reading this chapter, do you think that CVs you've designed in the past do enough to address the issue of engaging with and overcoming competition? How do you think you can better your previous efforts? Use the space below to jot down any ideas that have occurred to you.

_____

_____

_____

_____

_____

_____

_____

_____

_____

One of the biggest criticisms employers have about the CVs they receive is that there is nothing in them that is relevant to the position for which the candidate is applying. In terms of what you have done in the past, do you think that this criticism could be levelled at you? If so, what do you plan to do to address the criticism when you next need a CV?

_____

_____

_____

_____

_____

_____

_____

_____

_____

With CVs you have designed in the past, are you satisfied that you paid enough attention to bringing your strong points into prominence? With the benefit of hindsight, what could you have done better?

_____

_____

_____

_____

_____

_____

_____

_____

_____

_____

_____

ONLINE RESOURCE

The three As of successful job hunting

You can access a free download if you want to find out more about what it takes to be successful when it comes to tackling tough job markets.

The three As are the underpinnings of successful job hunting in the kind of conditions everyone has had to get used to in recent years. The three As are as follows:

Accessibility

When you apply for a job, an employer has got to be able to see what you have done and what you are capable of doing in a compressed period of time. What you have to say about yourself in your CV (and any cover letter you put with it) plays a key part in determining how you score in terms of accessibility. In a CV and cover letter, what's good about you has got to come over first time because it won't get another chance.

Availability

You need to be there when employers want to talk to you. You need to be someone who can be contacted on the phone or by email without any hassle. You need to be able to attend interviews on cue.

Application

Sometimes you strike lucky but, more often than not, getting the job you want comes at the end of a long hard slog with a few kicks in the teeth along the way. You need to have the staying power to stand up to this kind of treatment. Success is to keep going. Failure is to give way to feelings of disappointment and discouragement.

www.TYCoachbooks.com/CVs

5 CVS FOR MAILSHOTS

- Understand the reasons for sending out unsolicited CVs to employers (what you are hoping to achieve).
- Know how to put together a CV for this purpose.
- Know how to organize a mailshot.
- Know how to evaluate your success.

COACHING SESSION 30

What's the point?

Consider the following statement:

'Sending out an unsolicited CV to an employer has no purpose other than to reveal a snapshot. If they happen to have a suitable position for you at the time, great, but if they haven't then the CV is effectively dead and buried.'

What do you think of the statement? Is it true or not? Draw on your own experience to back up the answer you have given.

_____

_____

_____

_____

_____

_____

_____

THE AIM OF A MAILSHOT

Sending a copy of your CV to selected employers along with a suitably worded cover letter is one way of accessing the elusive invisible job market, including:

- jobs that aren't advertised
- jobs that, for one reason or another, employers keep to themselves
- jobs that are rumoured to be the best jobs.

But first let's consider the aim: what are you hoping to achieve by sending an unsolicited CV to an employer who has probably never heard of you before?

The answer is that you are hoping to strike lucky. More precisely, you are hoping that your CV will land on the right desk at the right time:

- The **right desk** means the desk of whoever in the organization is responsible for hiring people like you.
- The **right time** means the time when there is a need to recruit someone with your blend of skills and experience – or a need is about to arise.

Failing this, what you want to ensure is that your CV is put away in the **right file**. The right file is the one that gets revisited when a vacancy does arise and this acts as yet another reminder that employers often look back at previous applicants *before* considering other methods of recruitment.

They do this because recruitment is, on the whole, an expensive and time-consuming process. Advertising and paying the fees of people like recruitment consultants costs a lot of money. Sifting through large numbers of applicants and then whittling them down into an interview list and a shortlist can take several weeks before yielding any results. By contrast, a previous applicant can be contacted quickly by phone and, if all goes well, someone could be offered the job in the space of a few days. The total cost is next to nothing – which is great news, especially at a time when employers' budgets are tight!

 COACH'S TIP

Unexpected rewards

Sending out an unsolicited CV can achieve a great deal more than just revealing a snapshot of current vacancies. Employers often hold on to CVs that take their interest for long periods of time. You could find to your surprise that you get a phone call out of the blue months or even years later.

WHAT'S IN IT FOR YOU?

While sending off unsolicited CVs seems, on the face of it, a hit-and-miss way of sourcing suitable job opportunities, it can work and often with spectacular results. Consider the following:

- In most cases you won't be up against hundreds of other applicants. A trawl through CVs that employers have found interesting and kept on file will, at best, yield only a handful of people. Indeed, you could even find yourself in the enviable position of being the only candidate called in for an interview. This is no guarantee you will get the job, of course, but at least you won't have the challenge of having to think up ways of making yourself stand out from competitors.

- Your CV could just spark off enough interest to get an employer thinking: 'Could we create a slot for this person?'

- In recessionary times, employers often hold back before hiring. The job will still be there but they need something to give them a push. An unsolicited CV sent in by a candidate who ticks all the boxes could be all it takes.

THE TASK YOUR CV HAS TO PERFORM

So far so good, but employers receive hundreds of unsolicited CVs and it has to be said that most of them finish up in places where they will never see the light of day again! This begs the question: what can you do to make your CV interesting to the employers you have chosen to send it to? Where is the fine line drawn between CVs that are kept on file and those that are fed into the shredding machine?

Where jobs have been advertised in the press or on websites, you have the advantage of knowing what attributes employers are seeking in candidates, so, when it comes to the job of designing your CV, you can pick out areas where you have something to offer that will make them sit up and take note. However, with a mailshot, you have nothing to tell you what employers view as important attributes and what, therefore, they will find interesting about you.

The dictum that 'no one size fits all' is again the place to start. What interests one employer won't necessarily interest another, so, if you choose to deal with the problem by sending out the same standard version of your CV to everyone, you are missing the point.

COACHING SESSION 31

How would you deal with this problem?

Can you think of any ideas? Jot them down here:

_____

_____

_____

_____

_____

_____

_____

_____

_____

_____

_____

_____

_____

_____

_____

_____

_____

_____

_____

_____

_____

Here is a short case study.

CASE STUDY: MATT

Matt is a design engineer. Since he graduated five years ago, Matt has worked for a firm that designs, builds and installs special-purpose machinery used in the food-processing industry. Matt's firm is being forced to cut back after the cancellation of a major contract and staff are already being laid off. Matt has plans to get married next year and he and his fiancée have recently taken out a mortgage on a flat. Matt realizes therefore that he needs to start putting out some feelers on the job market. With this in mind, he decides to send his CV to five leading machinery manufacturers in the area where he lives.

Why will these five firms be interested in Matt? For a start, of course, there is his experience in designing special-purpose machines, but, with a little research, he might be able to find something else to say about himself in his cover letter and CV – something that these five firms will also find interesting. For example, has Matt had experience in using the same computer-aided design software that these firms use? If he has, then, yes, they are going to find this interesting. Similarly, they will find it interesting if Matt has worked on projects similar to the kinds of projects that pass through their design offices.

So how does Matt go about researching the five firms he has selected for his mailing list?

Websites

Websites are an obvious place to start. In Matt's case, he may, for example, be able to find out more about what kind of machines his five firms make. What do their websites have to say? Do they specialize? Do they build machines similar to the ones that Matt has worked on? If so, this aspect of his experience is something he can bring into prominence in the design of his CV.

Professional networks

Websites apart, people like Matt usually have other sources of useful information at their fingertips. Here is a checklist for him to consider:

- Does he know anyone who has ever worked for any of these firms? If so, what can they tell him?

- Is there anyone in his wider circle of contacts who could provide him with some useful insights?

- Does he have any links with bodies such as trade associations? Does he go to events such as industry fairs?

- Does his current employer compete for business with any of these five firms? If so, Matt's colleagues in sales could be a mine of information on how they operate.

This list is not exhaustive, but the point is this: it often takes no more than a few phone calls to extend your knowledge of the employers you have put on your mailing list. In this way, you can start to form a view of what there is about you that will interest them.

THE 'ONE QUICK READ' TEST AGAIN

Going back to the point that employers are bombarded with unsolicited CVs, something else to note is that a large number of them are from people who are completely unsuitable. The result is that unsolicited CVs receive a similar kind of treatment to spam emails. At best, they get a quick glance, so there is even more reason why what you have to say about yourself has to come across first time. Once again, to do this, the bulleted list in your cover letter and on the front page of your CV has got to register with the employer as something that is relevant to them. Clearly, a CV that you've pulled off the pile that you keep on the shelf in the spare room won't do the trick.

With an unsolicited CV, what is interesting about you again needs to be given prominent billing in your cover letter and on the front page of your CV (in your 'key skills/achievements' section again). It needs to be apparent to the reader that what you're saying about yourself is directed at them and not something you say to everyone.

COACHING SESSION 32

Harry's cover letter

Below is an example of a cover letter. It is typical of many that employers receive.

Do you have any thoughts on Harry's cover letter? What are its good and bad points?

Good points

_____

_____

_____

Bad points

_____

_____

_____

Harry Hopeful
1 Watermill Close
Upton-on-Creek
UPXX 9XX

Tel: xxxx xxxxxx
Mobile: xxxxxxx xxxx
Email: harryhopeful@xxi.com

1 February 2014

Human Resources Manager
Cockle & Whelk Seafoods Limited
Riverside Industrial Estate
Upton-on-Creek
UPXX 8XX

Dear Sir/Madam

I am writing to see whether you have any suitable vacancies for me. A copy of my CV is enclosed from which you will see that:

- I am a 29-year-old graduate with a degree in food technology
- I have three years' experience of working for a major supplier of frozen foods (including seafoods)
- Two of these three years have been spent in customer service and quality control
- I live locally.

I am available for an interview at any time.

Yours faithfully

Harry Hopeful

Harry Hopeful
Enc.: CV

There are a number of good points about Harry's letter:

- It is well written and concise.
- He has made an effort to bring in information that the recipient will find relevant.
- He has put the information in a prominent place (in his cover letter).

However, what Harry hasn't done is to make it clear to Cockle & Whelk Seafoods what kind of opportunity he is seeking. The impression that his letter gives is that he will be interested in anything that they have to offer – which may or may not be the case. What we don't know, of course, is whether or not he has been any clearer about his ambitions in the main body of his CV.

The danger for Harry is that, if his letter has the effect that he intends, Cockle & Whelk Seafoods will be on the phone or sending him an email inviting him to come in for an interview. This is fine, if Harry happens to be out of work or his job is at risk, but what if this isn't the case? What if, for example, the object of sending the CV was to see whether Cockle & Whelk could pay him a better salary than the one he is earning currently? What if he goes to the interview and finds it's a complete waste of time because Cockle & Whelk's salary scales are no improvement on where he is working now?

When you're sending off a mailshot to employers who have no previous knowledge of you, it is important to make sure your CV and the cover letter that goes with it say enough about you to enable readers to form an opinion on whether they have anything to interest you or not.

COACHING SESSION 33

Jane Excellent sends out her CV for a mailshot

Take a look at this example of a CV for a mailshot. This time Jane Excellent, the fictitious applicant, has designed the CV to send out to six large firms in her area to see whether they have any openings for top-flight PAs. Pick out what you see as the good and bad points in the example CV. Compare it with the CV Jane Excellent designed to apply for a job where she knew she would be up against competition (see Coaching session 29).

Good points

_____

_____

Bad points

_____

_____

_____

Curriculum Vitae

Name	Jane Excellent
Address	Flat 4
	Quayside House
	River Street
	PORTCHESTER-ON-SEA
	PC2 1AA
Email	janee@xxx.com
Telephone	Home xxxxx xxxxxx (after 6 p.m. – except Thursday)
	Office xxxxx xxxxxx
	Mobile xxxxx xxxxxx

Key skills/achievements

- I have a good employment record with ten years' experience of working as a Secretary/PA at a senior level.
- I have a high level of IT proficiency and I am fully conversant with all versions of Microsoft Word, Excel, PowerPoint and other leading packages.
- I can do shorthand up to 100 wpm.
- I am fully flexible. I have no ties and I am used to working long and unsociable hours.
- I have D32/D33 assessor qualifications.

Education

1981–1987	City Comprehensive School
1987–1990	Queens' Commercial College (part-time day release)
2000–2005	Portchester College of Further Education (evenings)

Qualifications

GCE O level: English Language (B), Business Studies (B), Geography (C) Art (D) 1987

RSA Typewriting: Stages 1, 2 and 3 (1987–1990)

RSA English Language: Stages 1, 2 and 3 (1987–1990)

Pitman Shorthand: 90 and 100 wpm (1988–1990)

RSA Word Processing: Stages 1, 2 and 3 (1999–2000)

RSA Teachers' Diploma in Administration Skills (2002)

D32/33 Assessors' Awards (2002)

RSA/OCR Integrated Business Technology Stage 3 (2005)

IT Skills

I am fully conversant with all versions of Microsoft Word, Excel, Access, PowerPoint and Publisher.

Ambitions

I am seeking a position as a Secretary/PA in a larger organization where I will be working with a wider cross-section of people.

Salary

I currently earn £30k per annum. I am seeking a salary of £35k minimum.

Employment history

1995–present   Portchester Building Supplies Limited

Position held: Secretary/PA to Managing Director. In addition to secretarial duties I have responsibility for payroll and IT.

1988–1994   Martin & Associates

Position held: Administration Assistant in a small firm of solicitors. Telephone calls, correspondence, word processing letters, legal documents etc. using Microsoft Word (initially self-taught). Reason for leaving: to pursue ambition to become a Secretary/PA.

1987–1988   Furnival and Sons Limited

12 months' placement with firm of paper merchants. General office duties: typing, filing, inputting data etc. Reason for leaving: end of placement.

Period of notice
One month

Nationality
British

Health
Good (non-smoker)

Leisure-time activities
Swimming. Going to the theatre. Keeping fit – I visit the gym twice a week.

References

Work: Graham Martin, Senior partner, Martin & Associates (Tel: xxxx xxxx)

Personal: June Griffiths, Senior Lecturer in Computer Studies, Portchester College of Further Education (Tel: xxxx xxxx)

HOW TO ORGANIZE A MAILSHOT

When you send out unsolicited CVs, you're never quite certain how much interest they will generate. On the one hand, you may hear nothing; on the other, you may find yourself inundated with requests to go to interviews. If you are unemployed or a student or in a situation where your employer is happy to let you have time off work to go to interviews because your job is at risk, this won't be a problem. However, if you're like most people and interviews have to be fitted in by making excuses or taking odd days of leave that are owing to you, you could find yourself facing some difficult choices. The solution is simple: unless you're desperate to make a move, send your CVs out in small batches.

 COACH'S TIP

The initial lack of response isn't necessarily a bad sign

Sending off a CV and hearing nothing is usually taken as a bad sign (the CV wasn't read or, if it was, it didn't succeed in sparking any interest). What you mustn't forget, though, is that one of the aims of an unsolicited CV is for the recipient to retain it (in the right file). Sometimes you will be told when this happens but usually you won't. It will only become apparent weeks, months or even years later when you get a phone call or an email out of the blue.

Target your mailshot

The tendency for people to pepper employers with unsolicited CVs extends to the apparent randomness with which they do it. They send their CVs to 'anybody and everybody' in the wild hope that, by an act of pure chance, one will find its mark. This contrasts with a targeted approach – picking out employers who hire people like you and doing this by finding out more about your own particular sector of the job market. Here is where job ads are a good source of information on what kind of people employers are hiring. Keep your eye on them.

Send your CV to the right person

Harry Hopeful addressed his cover letter to the HR Manager of Cockle & Whelk Seafoods and, if you asked him why, he would probably tell you that, in most organizations, HR managers are responsible for recruitment.

☺☺ COACHING SESSION 34

The right person

From your knowledge of how organizations work, do you have any views on who would be the best person to send an unsolicited CV to? You don't have an ad to tell you what to do, so whom would you choose? Give your answer here and explain the thinking behind your choice.

_____

_____

_____

_____

_____

Unless you happen to be looking for a job in human resources, the right person won't be the HR Manager. For example, if you're an accountant, the decision on whether to hire you or not is ultimately going to be down to whoever heads up the finance end of the business. In other words, this is the person you need to be targeting with your unsolicited CV. What's more, there are two other problems attached to sending unsolicited CVs to HR Managers:

1. The chances are that they won't be experts in your field of work so what you have to say about yourself in your CV and cover letter might go straight over their heads.

2. HR managers have bigger piles of unsolicited CVs on their desks than anyone else, whereas people like Heads of Finance won't be nearly so inundated.

Unless you happen to know, it is worth making a phone call and asking for the **name of the person** who heads up the part of the organization in which you want to work. Sometimes an organization's website will give the names of its key figures.

Put together a cover letter

The cover letter that accompanies an unsolicited CV needs to be clear and concise. At a glance, the reader needs to be able to see:

- who you are
- what you have to offer (your list of bullet points)
- why you're writing to them (what you're seeking to achieve)
- how you can be contacted.

COACH'S TIP

Take care with cover letters

Sadly, most cover letters that accompany unsolicited CVs haven't had a lot of thought given to them. For example, it's not unusual to find a letter in a standard format where blank spaces have been left for writing in the employer's name and address. Don't do this. No one wants to feel they're part of a mailshot.

Mark the envelope 'confidential'

This is a good way of ensuring that the right pair of eyes reads your cover letter and CV.

Post vs. email

COACHING SESSION 35

Post or email?

With an unsolicited CV you have the choice of submitting it by email or putting it in the post. Given the aim of the exercise, what would you do? Explain why.

_____

_____

_____

_____

_____

With emails, busy people are selective about what they print off, so there is a danger that someone who has no current vacancies will simply delete what you send in. The result is that your CV doesn't end up where you want it to end up – in the right file.

Two other dangers are that:

■ your email is treated as spam and deleted without being read

■ the file attachment containing your CV isn't opened because of concerns about unleashing viruses into the organization's IT system.

COACH'S TIP

Play safe!

With an unsolicited CV, play safe and put it in the post. When it arrives at the other end, it will be in the form of hard copy – that is, in the form it needs to be if it's going to be put away in the right file.

WHAT IS SUCCESS?

If your speculative CV has had the good fortune to land on the right desk at the right time, then the chances are that you'll find out about it pretty quickly. The employer will be on the phone or sending you a letter or an email, and it won't be long before you're in front of them being interviewed. If, on the other hand, you hear nothing, then the difficulty is knowing what to read into the experience.

COACHING SESSION 36

What would you read into it?

Write your answer in the space below and say what, if anything, you would do about the lack of response.

_____

_____

_____

_____

_____

Don't expect a reply

Whether or not employers should write back to everyone who sends in a speculative CV is a matter of opinion. Some do, some don't, and this is a fact you are going to have to learn to live with. The mistake, however, is to view lack of response as not just a reflection of the employer's bad manners, but evidence of failure. For example, what happens in many cases is that a speculative CV succeeds in registering in the right way with the person who reads it but, because there are no suitable opportunities at that moment, it finishes up being put in the file that will come out the next time the employer has a vacancy. In other words, the CV has done its job but, because you hear nothing, you come away feeling that the exercise has been a waste of time. The problem is therefore the lack of feedback.

Without feedback, how do you measure the success of your mailshot? Did your CV do its job or didn't it? And, in terms of the design and content of your CV, how do you know whether you're getting it right or not?

Take stock

Measuring the success of unsolicited CVs is difficult, not just because of the lack of feedback but also because a lot hinges on how much your blend of skills and experience is in demand at a particular point in time – something not easy to gauge. However, if you're getting no joy at all from your speculative mailshots other than the occasional acknowledgement letter, then it may be time to pause and take stock. Are you doing anything wrong? Here is a short checklist that may help you to pinpoint the problem:

- Are you picking out the wrong employers? Is your CV being sent to organizations that don't have much demand for people like you?

- Could your salary expectations be putting employers off? While there is nothing wrong with looking for a well-paid job, it goes without saying that you will find fewer takers if the salary you are seeking is over and above what someone in your line of work would normally expect to be paid.

- Are you difficult to contact? Could you be putting barriers in the way of employers who want to talk to you?

- Are you making the mistake of sending the same CV to everyone? Are you following the rule about customizing the CVs you send out? Are your CVs relevant to the needs of the employers you're canvassing?

- Are you following the same rules with your cover letters? From a quick glance at your cover letter, will an employer be able to see that you have something to offer that is relevant to them?

- Is your CV being sent to the right person – that is, the person responsible for hiring people like you?

NEXT STEPS

Sending out speculative mailshots can sometimes seem like a lot of effort for little result. However, if you do it properly, it can, and does, work. The rewards for you are:

- connecting with opportunities that haven't yet surfaced on the job market

- making sure unadvertised opportunities stay that way because you got in first.

The next chapter (Chapter 6) looks at designing CVs for agencies (recruitment consultants). Agencies offer another way of accessing the invisible job market, but here the challenge is designing a CV that will ignite the interest of someone who will have very different motives from those of an employer. The secret to success with agencies is tapping into what drives them, and to do this you have to start by understanding them and how they operate.

TAKEAWAYS

Has reading this chapter given you any useful ideas for attacking the invisible job market – anything you hadn't considered previously? Jot them down in the space below.

_____

_____

_____

_____

_____

_____

_____

_____

_____

Has the point about making sure to customize speculative CVs caused you to revise your ideas? What will you be doing in future that you haven't done in the past?

_____

_____

_____

_____

_____

_____

_____

_____

_____

_____

_____

Have you learned anything useful about how to organize a speculative mailshot? List the main points.

_____

_____

_____

_____

_____

_____

_____

_____

_____

Given that employers are inundated with unsolicited emails, what have you learned from reading this chapter that will make your CV one of the ones that doesn't get treated as spam? Sum up what you have learned.

_____

_____

_____

_____

_____

_____

_____

_____

_____

As a result of reading this chapter, have you revised your opinions about the value of speculative mailshots? How have your opinions changed?

_____

_____

_____

_____

_____

_____

_____

_____

_____

Have your ideas changed on how to judge the success of speculative job applications? In what ways have your ideas changed?

_____

_____

_____

_____

_____

_____

_____

_____

_____

_____

_____

ONLINE RESOURCE

The growth of the invisible job market

You can access a free download if the subject of the growth of the invisible job market interests you.

The classic way to fill a vacant position was to advertise it as widely as possible, so that:

- anyone interested could apply

- the employer had a choice of candidates.

In contrast, the invisible job market concerns the jobs that are found through networking and direct contact. The invisible job market has always been there but the signs are that it has flourished in recent times, for several reasons.

The main one is the time and resources it takes to run advertisements, sift through applications and carry out interviews. Even then, there is no guarantee of finding anyone suitable. More to the point, time and resources are in short supply when the trend for many has been for more and more work to be placed in fewer and fewer pairs of hands. What has happened is that managers do what they always do when they're put under pressure. They look for short cuts.

But this isn't the whole story. Two other forces are at work that have influenced the growth of the invisible job market:

1. An increasingly important part of today's employment scene is made up of knowledge and/or technology-based organizations, which see their people needs in terms of 'something special'.

2. Many employers worry that bringing in someone new could result in introducing a poor performer or a 'bad apple'. Here, the concern is the risks attached to exiting people – ranging from the damage such people could inflict on the business through to the cost of dealing with litigation that could arise from a dismissal.

But how do these perceptions of the difficulties that surround the recruitment of staff affect the way employers behave in the job market? Let's now draw the threads together and see what picture emerges.

- There is a greater tendency for employers to 'hold fire' before automatically replacing leavers. This holding fire may be partly rationalized by 'seeing if we can manage'. The justification is in terms of trying to reduce costs rather than apprehension about the situations these employers see themselves getting into. The 'holding fire' may in turn manifest itself in the form of hiring a temp from an employment agency. In the fullness of time the temp may be offered the job (the well-known temp-to-perm transmutation).

- Employers are less inclined to use advertising as a means of filling vacancies. Advertising will be seen as 'too slow' or as unselective, i.e. attracting too many applicants of the wrong calibre who take time and effort to weed out.

- If the demand is for people with specialist or scarce skills, advertising may not be seen as the appropriate medium anyway. 'The kind of people we want won't be looking at job ads' is a remark we often hear from employers these days.

- Employers are increasingly using headhunters and recruitment consultants: people who can source candidates from their networks of contacts or from their files. Headhunters and recruitment consultants will also have the expertise that employers find reassuring.

- Companies want to avoid the pain of going through long-winded, time-consuming recruitment exercises by approaching people they directly or indirectly know.

Go through this list and you have the reasons for the growth of the so-called invisible market – the positions that are never advertised; the jobs that are so hard to find out about; the jobs that are often the best jobs.

Most of all, though, appreciate three important facts about the invisible job market:

- It's big.

- It's getting bigger.

- You need to get in on it.

www.TYCoachbooks.com/CVs

6 CVS FOR AGENCIES

✓ OUTCOMES FROM THIS CHAPTER

■ Know how to write and design a CV for the purpose of registering with agencies.

■ Understand what drives agencies and know how to make them perform for you.

■ Recognize, in career terms, what you can gain from engaging with agencies.

■ Know how to create a well-crafted CV that will help to ensure that it is your name that comes out in the file searches.

HOW AGENCIES WORK

It has to be said that dealing with agencies can be quite trying, but, at the end of the day, the only real measure of their effectiveness is how good (or bad) they are at coming up with the right jobs for you. Nothing else matters. But before you sit down to the job of designing a CV to send off to an agency, it is important first to understand what drives them.

Like any business, an employment agency is there to make money. However, in their case, they can do this only by making successful placements. If they place someone with one of their clients, they will charge a fee (this varies from one agency to the next). This arrangement is known as 'no placement, no fee' and it is what attracts many employers to using agencies. They get to see a sample of who is out there on the market without it costing them anything – at least up to the point when they take someone on.

Not all agencies are the same but in many cases the people who work for them (recruitment consultants) are paid on commission. In turn, what this means is that:

■ their minds are highly focused on getting 'sales' (making placements)

■ candidates who are seen as 'easy to place' get the most attention

■ conversely, candidates who are seen as less easy to place can get put to one side

■ in the enthusiasm to chalk up sales, the finer points in candidates' instructions can get overlooked

■ candidates who come across as awkward or difficult to please are given a miss.

COACHING SESSION 37

What is your experience of dealing with agencies?

Here are some negative opinions about how agencies perform. They come from people whose experience has been bad. Put a tick alongside any where the opinion expressed is one you would share.

People who work in agencies are good at talking the talk but not so good when it comes to getting results. ☐

They push you into taking jobs that are totally unsuitable. ☐

They're only interested in the commission they're going to earn. ☐

They make no effort to look after your best interests. ☐

You put your name down with an agency then, in most cases, you never hear from them again. ☐

You can't trust anything they say – 90 per cent of it is sales talk with nothing to back it up. ☐

A lot of agencies are temp-orientated. They're not so hot when it comes to finding permanent jobs. ☐

You never deal with the same person twice, so you have to keep explaining yourself over and over again to the point where you end up tearing your hair out. ☐

They have no concept of what you do for a living, so how can you possibly have any confidence in their ability to act properly on your behalf? ☐

On the face of it, agencies are (ultimately) an expensive option for employers, which begs the question of why they nonetheless use them.

👥 COACHING SESSION 38

Why do employers use agencies?

Drawing on your own experience, what do you think attracts employers to using agencies? Why are employers prepared to pay the big fees agencies charge?

Give your answer here.

_____

_____

_____

_____

_____

_____

Employers have different reasons for using agencies, but by and large they fall into the following categories:

- **Employers in a hurry.** This is where the need to find someone to fill a vacant slot is urgent – for example, a key member of staff has departed at a critical time and the employer needs to get someone on board quickly or the business will suffer. In such circumstances, going down the usual route of placing advertisements and sifting through dozens of applications won't appeal because of the time constraints. An agency, on the other hand, has the capacity to carry out a file search straight away and at no cost to the employer. In 24 to 48 hours the same employer can have a pile of CVs sitting on his or her desk.

- **Employers who feel that advertising does not work for them.** Advertising is a costly business and one where the outcome isn't guaranteed. An employer can spend a large sum of money on advertising and find that, at the end of it, they have nothing to show for it. None of the applicants who've replied are suitable, so, as far as filling their vacancy is concerned, they're no further forward than when they started. By contrast, using an agency means that employers can have a preview of who is out there on the market without it costing them anything.

- **Employers without the resources.** Employers, especially smaller ones, may not have the resources or expertise to comb through dozens of job applications and embark on the process of sorting the wheat from the chaff. Agencies offer a solution.

COACH'S TIP

Don't pass agencies by

Dealing with agencies can be painful, but they provide a gateway to parts of the job market that would otherwise be closed to you. Disengaging from agencies is therefore a mistake. Rather, see the challenge as getting agencies to perform for you and, at the same time, see the crafting of your CV as an important part of this challenge.

This short introduction to what goes on behind the scenes in employment agencies is not intended to confirm your worst fears or put you off using them. Rather, the idea is to focus your mind on the task you face when you design a CV to send to an agency.

HOW TO PUT TOGETHER A CV FOR AN AGENCY

This time, the task your CV has to perform is different. The people who will be reading it will be people who see a lot of CVs but who won't be looking at it in the same way as an employer would.

COACHING SESSION 39

The agency CV

What do you see as the big differences between a CV that's going to an agency and one where the purpose is to send it directly to an employer (either in response to an advertisement or in the form of a mailshot)?

Record your thoughts here.

_____

_____

_____

_____

_____

_____

_____

In the case of a CV that you're putting together for the purpose of sending it to an agency, what you need to have your mind focused on is doing whatever it takes to make sure that:

- it's your name that comes out in the file searches
- you connect with the right opportunities.

There are thus three important facts to consider before you sit down to the job of designing a CV for an agency. These are as follows:

1. As previously mentioned, people who work in employment agencies are highly focused on results. Your value in their eyes can be understood quite simply in terms of whether they can place you in a job or not.

2. Your CV will be one of many the agency receives, so, again, the 'one quick read' test comes into play.

3. In many agencies, a file search is carried out by computer or by people who may not have a complete understanding of what you do or the terminology or jargon you use.

Your marketable talents

What gets a recruitment consultant's blood racing? Based on what you have learned already about what drives people who work in agencies, the parts of your portfolio you need to highlight are those that pick you out as someone they can sell to their clients. Is this where you hit a snag? After all, you don't know their client list, so how can you even guess at which of your personal attributes/areas of experience they are going to find most interesting? What should you be saying about your key skills and achievements on the front page of your CV?

What do agencies' clients find interesting? The answer to this question can be found by going back to what kind of employers use agencies – what kind of situations they're in and what in, in candidate terms, they're hoping the agency can provide.

 COACH'S TIP

Catch the agency's eye

Make sure that your CV front page shows aspects of your skills or experience that will be an 'easy sell' to their clients.

COACHING SESSION 40

The agency CV front page

What are your thoughts on this? Without any inkling of what the agency's clients see as important qualities in the people they hire, how do you go about designing your front page?

Use the space below to write down your ideas.

_____

_____

_____

_____

_____

_____

_____

_____

_____

Here is a short checklist that may help you pinpoint which of your talents/areas of experience will find most favour when it comes to impressing your credentials on an employment agency:

- Do you have any scarce skills or unusual areas of experience? Employers who ask for help from agencies often do so because they feel that they're looking for someone special and that, for this reason, other methods of recruitment may not work for them.

- Look to anything in your background that identifies you as a 'safe pair of hands'. Employers frequently go to agencies because they're looking for someone to steady the ship after a period of turbulence. For example: experience of dealing with the aftermath of a major restructuring exercise would be good to mention.

- Can you claim to have any first-hand knowledge of any technique, process, item of equipment, software application, etc. that could conceivably be described as 'new'? Employers often turn to agencies when they have made investments in state-of-the-art technology and need to bring skills and know-how into the organization that they don't yet have in-house.

MAKE SURE AGENCIES UNDERSTAND YOU

It is important that agencies understand you because, if they don't, you will find them phoning you up about opportunities that don't interest you.

COACHING SESSION 41

The importance of clarity

To illustrate the point, here is another case study for you to consider.

Case study: Liam

Since leaving school ten years earlier, Liam has spent his entire career working for one employer – a leading manufacturer of white goods – where, after serving an apprenticeship, he took on a role in maintenance. Liam is now 27 and he has decided the time has come for him to make a move. In doing this, he feels he is not in a hurry and that it is just a case of waiting for the right job to come along. In terms of what he wants to do next, he has set his sights on getting into the field of commissioning and installing new machinery where he feels his knowledge of robotics and automated assembly lines will stand him in good stead. What's more, working on commissioning and installation will give him the opportunity to travel and see more of the world.

With this aim in mind, Liam sends his CV off to an agency that specializes in technical appointments. What he finds, however, is that the agency is on the phone every few days wanting to talk about jobs in maintenance that have just come on to their books. Each time Liam speaks to a different person and each time he goes to great pains to explain that he is not looking for another job in maintenance. Nonetheless, the calls keep coming until finally Liam loses patience and tells the agency not to ring him any more.

What lessons do you think you can learn from Liam's experience? Use the space below to list them in bullet-point form.

_____

_____

_____

_____

_____

_____

Reading between the lines of Liam's case study, it looks as if, when putting together his CV, he didn't make it sufficiently clear to the agency what he wanted them to do for him. They responded in the way all agencies tend to do when they're not given direction. They locked on to what they saw as Liam's most marketable feature (his experience in maintenance) and then proceeded to pepper him with everything that came on to the books that offered a match. In fairness, Liam tried to explain why the jobs in maintenance didn't interest him, but for some reason the message didn't get through.

The case study illustrates the importance of making sure that agencies understand you and what happens when they don't. Apart from the waste of their time, agencies get fed up with candidates who keep saying no. The effort that goes into trying to place them diminishes. The calls stop.

How do you get your message across? The ambitions section of your CV is the obvious place to spell out what kind of opportunities you are seeking but what you also need to consider are the following:

- A **good cover letter** to go with your CV – one in which the message about where you want to go next is repeated
- Setting out your ambitions in **concise** and **unambiguous** language.

 COACH'S TIP

Keep your goal in mind

Remember what you are trying to achieve. If a job comes on to the agency's books which is right up your street, you want to be sure that you trigger the retrieval systems. The file search has got to throw out your name.

◯◯ COACHING SESSION 42

Jane Excellent sends her CV to an agency

Using the fictitious Jane Excellent again, look at the example of a CV she has designed to send to three employment agencies that specialize in top-drawer appointments for secretaries and PAs.

What do you see as the good points in the example? Compare it with the two other CVs Jane put together (see Coaching sessions 29 and 33).

_____

_____

_____

_____

_____

_____

_____

_____

_____

_____

_____

_____

_____

_____

_____

_____

_____

_____

_____

Curriculum Vitae

Name   Jane Excellent

Address   Flat 4
                    Quayside House
                    River Street
                    PORTCHESTER-ON-SEA
                    PC2 1AA

Email   janee@xxx.com

Telephone   Home xxxxx xxxxxx (after 6 p.m. – except Thursday)
                    Office xxxxx xxxxxx
                    Mobile xxxxx xxxxxx

Key skills/achievements

- I have ten years' experience of working as a Secretary/PA at a senior level.
- I am qualified to RSA Stage 3 in typewriting, word-processing and English.
- I hold Pitman qualifications in shorthand up to 100 wpm.
- I have a high level of IT proficiency and I am fully conversant with all versions of Microsoft Word, Excel, PowerPoint and other leading packages.
- I hold D32/D33 assessor qualifications

Education

1981–1987	City Comprehensive School
1987–1990	Queens' Commercial College (part-time day release)
2000–2005	Portchester College of Further Education (evenings)

Qualifications

GCE O level: English Language (B), Business Studies (B), Geography (C) Art
(D) 1987

RSA Typewriting: Stages 1, 2 and 3 (1987–1990)

RSA English Language: Stages 1, 2 and 3 (1987–1990)

Pitman Shorthand: 90 and 100 wpm (1988–1990)

RSA Word Processing: Stages 1, 2 and 3 (1999–2000)

RSA Teachers' Diploma in Administration Skills (2002)

D32/33 Assessors' Awards (2002)

RSA/OCR Integrated Business Technology Stage 3 (2005)

IT skills

I am fully conversant with all versions of Microsoft Word, Excel, Access, PowerPoint and Publisher.

Employment history

1995–present   Portchester Building Supplies Limited

Position held: Secretary/PA to Managing Director. In addition to secretarial duties I have responsibility for payroll and IT.

1988–1994   Martin & Associates

Position held: Administration Assistant in a small firm of solicitors. Telephone calls, correspondence, word processing letters, legal documents etc. using Microsoft Word (initially self-taught),. Reason for leaving: to pursue ambition to become a Secretary/PA.

1987–1988   Furnival and Sons Limited

12 months' placement with firm of paper merchants. General office duties: typing, filing, inputting data etc. Reason for leaving: end of placement.

Ambitions

I am seeking a position as a Secretary/PA in a larger organization where I will be working with a wider cross-section of people.

Salary

I currently earn £30k per annum. I am seeking a salary of £35k minimum.

Period of notice

One month

Nationality

British

Health

Good (non-smoker)

Leisure-time activities

Swimming. Going to the theatre. Keeping fit – I visit the gym twice a week.

References

Work: Graham Martin, Senior partner, Martin & Associates (Tel: xxxx xxxx)

Personal: June Griffiths, Senior Lecturer in Computer Studies, Portchester College of Further Education (Tel: xxxx xxxx)

Contrary to everything you've learned so far about customizing CVs, putting together a CV for one agency is no different from putting together a CV for another. You can therefore use a standard model in the way Jane Excellent did in this example.

NEXT STEPS

This chapter has looked at the task you face when you're called on to design a CV to send to an agency. The task this time is different because of the need to engage with the forces that drive people who work in agencies, namely:

- success in terms of placements

- the financial rewards that go with it.

To make your CV stand out from the hundreds that agencies receive every week, what you need to focus on is what it is about you that will sell. Not to put too fine a point on it, recruitment consultants need to see that they can make money out of you and the job of your CV is to show them how.

We have also stressed how important it is to keep consultants on the track you want them to follow and not one that is dictated by their desire to chalk up more sales. Communicating your aims and ambitions is the job of your CV. Nowhere is this more important than when you are dealing with an agency.

The book started with the premise that a CV is there to do what you want it to do – which may well have nothing to do with shopping around for jobs or getting interviews or any of the other tasks that CVs are normally expected to perform. A growing number of people earn their living independently, selling their skills and expertise to whoever happens to have a need for them and doing it either on their own or in partnership with others. The next chapter enters the world of people who work for themselves and examines the challenge of designing CVs for tasks that fall outside the mainstream.

👍 TAKEAWAYS

What's your experience of using agencies to access the job market? Having read this chapter, do you think there is anything you can do to get them to perform better for you? Write down your thoughts.

_____

_____

_____

_____

_____

_____

_____

_____

_____

_____

From reading this chapter, have you learned anything new about how agencies operate? Is the information useful to you? What do you know now that you didn't know previously?

_____

_____

_____

_____

_____

_____

_____

_____

_____

_____

_____

In the same way, what have you learned about the reasons why employers use agencies? Again, did you find the information useful?

_____

_____

_____

_____

_____

_____

_____

_____

_____

After reading this chapter, have you given any thought to identifying your marketable talents? In what ways will you use this approach to designing a CV for an agency?

_____

_____

_____

_____

_____

_____

_____

_____

_____

_____

What other new ideas will you incorporate into your agency CV?

_____

_____

_____

_____

_____

_____

_____

_____

_____

Did you find the section on making sure agencies understand you useful in the light of any experience that you have had? Note down any points that made a particular impression on you.

_____

_____

_____

_____

_____

_____

_____

_____

_____

_____

_____

7 CVS FOR BUSINESS

PEOPLE WHO WORK FOR THEMSELVES

It's not just people active on the job market who need a CV. People who work for themselves are occasionally asked to produce one – though, in their case, for different reasons.

🗪 COACHING SESSION 43

Creating a CV for business

Here is an example of someone who works independently and who is called on to produce a CV.

Case study: Suchada

Suchada is a mentor and she is currently seeking to expand her client list by selling the benefits of mentoring to a number of businesses she has targeted. It is the CEO of one of these businesses who expresses an interest in the service Suchada offers and wants to talk further. However, before committing himself to setting up a meeting, he wants to see a copy of Suchada's CV.

1. In your opinion, what is the task Suchada's CV needs to perform if it is going to work for her? Write your answer here:

_____

_____

_____

_____

_____

_____

_____

2. What in precise terms needs to go in Suchada's CV that will help convince her prospective new client that she will be a good person to do business with? Conversely, what is irrelevant (what does she need to leave out)?

_____

_____

_____

_____

_____

_____

_____

_____

Before the CEO of Suchada's prospective client engages her to mentor his management team, he will need to see that she is **competent** to do the job. In particular, he will need to see that:

- she is qualified to be a mentor
- she has experience of mentoring people at a senior level
- she has a proven track record
- she can deliver (she will be there when she's needed).

It is evidence of these competencies that needs to come across in her CV. Straight away, you will see the task that Suchada's CV has to perform will be very different from the one it would have to perform if she were applying for a job.

It is interesting to reflect on the concerns of people like the CEO of Suchada's prospective new client – concerns such as how consistent and reliable she is going to be. For example, if Suchada has not been in business for long, it would be a concern that she might be in it only for the short term. She might be offering the mentoring service as a fill-in while she is looking for a job in whatever field of work she came from originally. If so, what happens when she finds a job? The mentoring service would presumably cease and, from the CEO's point of view, this wouldn't be good.

People who work independently and who need a CV to enable them to source business have to address concerns such as these. In the case of Suchada, what this might mean is including enough information in her CV to explain:

- why she went into business as a mentor
- how she is getting on
- her long-term commitment to the role.

HOW TO PUT TOGETHER A CV TO SOURCE WORK

COACHING SESSION 44

What needs to go into a CV to source work?

Look at the framework version of your own CV and put yourself in the position of someone who works for themselves and who needs to design a CV to help them source work. What do you see as the main areas you need to focus on? List your thoughts here:

_____

_____

_____

_____

_____

_____

_____

_____

_____

Key skills/achievements

This is the section of your CV that:

- features on the front page
- says what there is to say about you that the reader of your CV will find most relevant and interesting.

It is reasonably safe to assume that someone who has asked to see your CV will at least give it the benefit of a reading, so, in one respect at least, a CV designed for business won't have to face such an uphill struggle as a CV designed for other purposes. What is important, however, is that you reach out to whomever it is you're seeking to impress – you do this by picking out areas of your portfolio that they will see as relevant. Suchada, for example, needs to pick out areas that would be relevant to the role of providing a mentoring service. The fact that she has been in business for a number of years and that, during that time, she has built up an impressive client list would be relevant to someone thinking about engaging her services.

Personal profile/ambitions

In this section it would be good to explain why you chose to go into business on your own account (the reason). At the same time, make it clear that you intend to carry on doing what you do to lay to rest any concerns that you may not be in it for the long term. Define your ambition in terms of wanting to go on working for yourself. Make it clear that you get your kicks out of providing your clients with a good service. In other words, let the reader of your CV see that:

- you like what you do
- you went into it for the right reasons
- you're not interested in doing anything else.

Salary

This section clearly has no relevance, so take it out.

Qualifications, education and training

Again, the test of relevance applies. In Suchada's case, this means that any qualifications she holds to practise as a mentor need to be included, whereas qualifications that have relevance only to the field she worked in previously should be relegated or, in some cases, left out altogether.

Employment history

Details of previous jobs and what you did in those jobs are only relevant if they reflect your competence to provide the service you are offering. Therefore, try as far as possible to present an overview of your employment history rather than going into a lot of detail.

Reason for leaving your last job

QQ COACHING SESSION 45

Your motivation

Put yourself in the position of someone who works for themselves and who is putting together a CV that will help them to source business. When it comes to giving the reason why you left your last job, what would you say? Here are two alternative explanations: A and B. Say why B is better than A and give your reasons.

A 'The branch where I was based closed down. I decided to start up on my own because nothing else was available.'

B 'I always wanted to work for myself because I felt I had the drive and energy to go it alone. When the branch where I worked closed down I saw it as an opportunity to put my belief to the test.'

_____

_____

_____

_____

_____

_____

_____

_____

_____

_____

Saying you left your last job because you made the decision to set up on your own demonstrates a lot of commitment and belief in yourself. You gave up a job with a regular income to take the plunge and go it alone. However, what if this wasn't the case and you went independent because your last job folded and you didn't have any other choice except to go on the dole?

Saying anything that might suggest that you're doing what you do now because you didn't have any other choice puts an unfortunate question mark over your motivation. Here, therefore, is where it might be better to say: yes, you did leave your last job because the business closed but you'd had in mind to go independent for some time anyway. The redundancy and the cash that went with it simply gave you the opportunity to do it.

COACHING SESSION 46

Jane Excellent goes it alone

Here is an example of a CV for business. In this case, Jane Excellent has decided to go it alone as a self-employed IT trainer. She gave notice to Portchester Building Supplies and left them six months ago. She has already built up a client list, but she is now looking for more business and she needs the CV for this purpose. Compare this CV to the other versions of Jane's CV you have looked at (Coaching sessions 29, 33 and 42).

Pick out the differences and list below what you see as the good points.

Differences

_____

_____

_____

_____

_____

Good points

_____

_____

_____

_____

_____

Curriculum Vitae

Name	Jane Excellent
Address	Flat 4
	Quayside House
	River Street
	PORTCHESTER-ON-SEA
	PC2 1AA
Email	janee@xxx.com
Telephone	Home xxxxx xxxxxx (after 6 p.m. – except Thursday)
	Office xxxxx xxxxxx
	Mobile xxxxx xxxxxx

Key skills/achievements

- I hold an RSA Teachers' Diploma in Administration Skills.
- I have D32/33 Assessor awards.
- I am able to train staff on most commercial packages including all versions of Microsoft Word, Excel, Access, PowerPoint and Publisher.
- I set up my own training business in August 2013 and I have already built up an impressive client list.
- I am fully flexible and able to meet a wide range of clients' needs. I am used to teaching mixed abilities, from graduates to people with disabilities and learning difficulties.

Education

1981–1987	City Comprehensive School
1987–1990	Queens' Commercial College (part-time day release)
2000–2005	Portchester College of Further Education (evenings)

Qualifications

GCE O level: English Language (B), Business Studies (B), Geography (C) Art (D) 1987

RSA Typewriting: Stages 1, 2 and 3 (1987–1990)

RSA English Language: Stages 1, 2 and 3 (1987–1990)

Pitman Shorthand: 90 and 100 wpm (1988–1990)

RSA Word Processing: Stages 1, 2 and 3 (1999–2000)

RSA Teachers' Diploma in Administration Skills (2002)

D32/33 Assessors' Awards (2002)

RSA/OCR Integrated Business Technology Stage 3 (2005)

Client list

I have carried out training and assessment assignments for the following leading clients:

- Highpoint Technologies Group
- Simmonds Construction Sealants plc
- Portchester Design Partnership
- Graphic Products Limited
- Avery & Sinclair plc

Employment history

1995–2013 Portchester Building Supplies Limited.

Position held: Secretary/PA to Managing Director. In addition to secretarial duties I had responsibility for payroll and IT. Reason for leaving: to set up in business as an IT trainer.

1988–1994 Martin & Associates

Position held: Administration Assistant in a small firm of solicitors. Telephone calls, correspondence, word processing letters, legal documents etc. using Microsoft Word (initially self-taught). Reason for leaving: to pursue ambition to become a Secretary/PA.

1987–1988 Furnival and Sons Limited

12 months' placement with firm of paper merchants. General office duties: typing, filing, inputting data etc. Reason for leaving: end of placement.

Period of notice

One month

Nationality

British

Health

Good (non-smoker)

Leisure-time activities

Swimming. Going to the theatre. Keeping fit – I visit the gym twice a week.

References

John Wedderburn, Sales Director, Simmonds Construction Sealants plc (Tel: xxxx xxxx)

Stella Reeves, Administration Manager, Graphic Products Limited (Tel: xxxx xxxx)

CVS TO PRESENT TO FINANCIAL INSTITUTIONS

People in business often have the need to borrow money, either to help them expand or to meet the cash-flow requirements that their businesses generate. For most people, this will mean going to the bank and asking for a loan or extending their overdraft facilities. Depending on the history of their relationship with the bank, they may be asked to back up their application by submitting a CV.

COACHING SESSION 47

What needs to go in a CV for a finance institution?

Here is a case study for you to consider. When you have read it, answer the question at the end.

Case study: Jack and Jill

After many years spent working in HR, Jack and Jill decided to go into business together running a small employment agency. They have now been going for just over two years and have arrived at the point where the small office that they initially rented is no longer big enough. At the same time, they need to invest in new hardware and software to bring their IT systems up to date. They realize that they are not going to be able to fund these projects out of their own pockets and that this means going to the bank and asking for a loan.

Put yourself in the position of the member of staff at Jack and Jill's bank who is responsible for vetting applications for loans from small businesses. What would you need to see to make you feel comfortable about advancing them a large sum of money? Give your answer below:

_____

_____

_____

_____

_____

_____

_____

_____

_____

Whether you will ever be called upon to provide a CV to back up an application for a loan or an overdraft, or to avail yourself of other financial services for business purposes, depends on your circumstances and, to some extent, on the luck of the draw. However, if you are put in this position, the CV you put together has to send out messages that:

- make the bank feel comfortable about granting you the facilities you want
- demonstrate your ability to manage your affairs effectively and prudently
- (in the case of a loan) show the bank that you will be able to repay it.

Key skills/achievements

Staying with the example of Jack and Jill, if the bank asks them to submit their CVs to support their application for a loan, then the achievements they need to focus on are the achievements of their business (i.e. what they have achieved as a result of working together as a team). As their CVs are directed at a bank, what will have the greatest impact is their record of financial achievement, so figures showing growth of turnover and profit would clearly be good to quote, for example. They could add to this any achievements in reducing debtor days, managing cash flow and repaying previous loans, etc.

A further point with business partnerships like Jack and Jill's is that what they say about themselves needs to be the same in both CVs. They need to come across as people who think the same way and whose prime concern is the performance of the business. Financial institutions have seen enough businesses fail because the people who run them no longer see eye to eye, so evidence of like-mindedness adds to the impression that Jack and Jill won't be falling out with each another (a possible consequence of which could be defaulting on the repayment of their loan).

Personal profile/ambitions

Ambitions need to be defined in terms of the ambitions of the business and, in Jack and Jill's case, their ambitions need to be seen as a team act (lots of 'we' and 'us' in place of 'I' and 'me'). In this respect, the bank should draw comfort from the fact that they are both on the same agenda. It bodes well for the longevity of the partnership and its ability to pay back the loan.

Salary

As before, take this section out because it isn't relevant.

Employment history

The example of Jack and Jill is interesting because what they did before they started their business (the time they spent in HR) is relevant and adds weight to their application. What might also be useful to include in this section are a few insights into how they came to start the business. For example, did they once work for the same firm? If so, it would show to the bank that their working together goes back a lot further than the start-up of the business. It adds to the impression that the partnership is stable and likely to be in place for the long term.

QUALIFICATIONS, EDUCATION AND TRAINING

Again, the example of Jack and Jill is interesting because many of the qualifications they gained while working in HR would have relevance to a 'people' business such as running an employment agency.

What else? With the reader of your CV in mind, it is important to identify anything that might come into conflict with what a financial institution such as a bank would see as a 'good risk'. One example might be if you have been in business before and, for some reason, the business ceased trading. Information such as this, taken in isolation, could send off alarm signals in the minds of financial institutions, so, if you are in this situation, you will need to pre-empt any concerns about your probity by adding information to your CV. This is a case of financial institutions always assuming the worst, unless they're told differently.

→ NEXT STEPS

It is common to find that people who work for themselves feel that they can go through life without ever having the need for a CV. However, what you have seen in this chapter is how the need can sometimes arise and, because it's not expected, it takes the individuals concerned by surprise. The result in many cases is that they're left having to start from scratch. They don't even have a framework version of their CV in place and, as a consequence, they end up putting something together quickly – something that is not consistent with their best efforts. Our message here is that CVs are for *everyone* – including people who don't fit into mainstream employment patterns.

Having looked at CVs under the various guises for which they are used, Chapter 8 considers how well-designed CVs can go on working for you. While a CV may be instrumental in getting you an interview, its impact on the selection process doesn't stop there. It can continue to play a major part in determining whether you get the job or not, and understanding how this happens is what you will be looking at next.

👍 TAKEAWAYS

Was it a surprise for you to learn that people who work for themselves are sometimes called upon to produce a CV? If you work for yourself, do you have a framework CV you could use if the need arose? If not, under what circumstances would you put one together?

_____

_____

_____

_____

_____

_____

_____

_____

If you work for yourself, have you ever had the experience of being asked to submit a CV to a prospective client? What have you learned from reading this chapter that will help you if you should find yourself in this position again?

_____

_____

_____

_____

_____

_____

_____

_____

Similarly, as a result of reading the chapter, would you proceed any differently if a bank (or other financial institution) asked you to submit a CV to support an application for an overdraft or a loan?

_____

_____

_____

_____

_____

_____

_____

_____

_____

If you are considering working for yourself – or if you already do – did you find the advice in this chapter about what to put in your framework CV useful? List any changes to your framework CV that you now plan to make.

_____

_____

_____

_____

_____

_____

_____

_____

_____

_____

Did the advice in this chapter about describing why you left your last job make you pause for thought? As a result, what changes do you plan to make to the design of your framework CV?

_____

_____

_____

_____

_____

_____

_____

_____

_____

8 HOW CVS GO ON WORKING FOR YOU

✔ OUTCOMES FROM THIS CHAPTER

- Understand the part your CV plays in steering your job applications to successful conclusions.
- Understand the benefits for you in revisiting your CV before you go for an interview.
- Recognize how consistency and credibility are linked together and why they are important.

COACHING SESSION 48

Revision questions

Here is a list of ten questions designed to act as a refresher on what you have learned so far from reading the book. Put your answer to each question in the space provided.

1. When is it permissible to send out the same CV more than once?

_____

_____

_____

2. What is the benefit for you in having a framework version of your CV already in place?

_____

_____

_____

3. What makes a CV interesting?

_____

_____

_____

4. Why is conciseness important?

_____

_____

_____

5. Why is it a bad idea to put a long list of outside interests in your CV?

_____

_____

_____

6. Why is it advisable to put an unsolicited CV in the post as opposed to emailing it?

_____

_____

_____

7. What is a CV for?

_____

_____

_____

8. Why is it important to make your personal ambitions clear?

_____

_____

_____

9. How do you measure the effectiveness of a CV?

_____

_____

_____

10. What is it important to do before you put the name of a referee in a CV?

_____

_____

_____

Is a CV just there to get you interviews? The answer is no, and in this chapter you will learn how a CV goes on working for you, not just at the interview stage but also up to the point where the final selection decision is made.

AT THE INTERVIEW

When you go to an interview, it is usual to find that the interviewer is sitting behind a desk with your CV and cover letter in front of him or her. If by this stage you have been asked to fill in an application form, this will also be on the interviewer's desk.

Except in cases where the interviewer has previous knowledge of you (for example, because you've worked for the same organization before), your cover letter, CV and any application form you've completed will tend to be the natural starting point for the dialogue that is about to open up. In this way, your cover letter, CV and application form will dictate:

- the direction of the interview
- the topics that come up for discussion
- the questions that are asked.

Interviewers vary enormously in terms of their experience and how much training they've been given. However, it is not uncommon to find that you are being interviewed by someone who is not used to sitting down in front of a complete stranger and trying to think up questions to ask. So what do interviewers like this do? The answer is that they are led by what's in front of them.

 COACH'S TIP

Your CV is a vital tool for the interviewer

Interviewers normally cast their eyes over candidates' cover letters, CVs and application forms shortly before the interview starts. The information they've just read is therefore freshest in their minds.

COACHING SESSION 49

A piece of advice

Consider the following advice:

> 'The best preparation for an interview is to revisit the CV you sent in when you applied for the job and the cover letter you put with it.'

Why is this good advice? Give your reason here:

_____

_____

_____

_____

_____

_____

_____

_____

_____

_____

_____

The power of your front page

On the front page of your CV and immediately after your personal information will be the list of your key skills and achievements. These, if you've done the job of designing your CV properly, will get the interview off to a good start. Your key skills and achievements are, of course, the strong areas of your application – what makes you a red-hot candidate for the job – so plenty of focus on these will go down well and the more you talk about them, the better.

To repeat one of the messages from earlier in the book, first impressions are important because these are the ones that carry forward (remember the 'halo effect'?), and nowhere is this more evident than at an interview. Getting the interview off to a flying start by talking about what makes you precisely the right candidate for the job will go a long way towards putting you on the road to getting the job.

COACHING SESSION 50

Should you take the lead?

One way of registering your strong points at the start of an interview might be to say to the interviewer: 'Shall I tell you a bit about myself?'

What's wrong with this approach? Explain why.

_____

_____

_____

_____

_____

_____

_____

With any interview you are, to a large extent, guessing where the focus of the interviewer's interest lies, so, by taking over an interview, you run the risk of setting off on a course that has little relevance as far as the interviewer is concerned. Our distinct advice here is: don't take over interviews. Instead, let the interviewer decide the direction the interview is going to take and in this way ensure that the direction is one that is relevant to the requirements of the job as the interviewer sees it. Leave it to interviewers to pick out the areas of your CV that they want to talk about. _Let your CV do the work for you._

Into the final few

Selection for most jobs involves attending more than one interview. Apart from small organizations, what tends to happen is that the first or preliminary interview is with someone like the company's HR Manager; then, at the next or shortlist stage, some of the candidates are brought back for an interview with the manager responsible for hiring people in the area of the business where the vacant position is located. What this means is that you will be seen by a fresh pair of eyes the second time round, so the business of making a good impression starts all over again. The point, however, is this. At each of the stages in the selection procedure your cover letter, CV and other documents are handed over from one interviewer to the next. They go on working for you. They will even be there at the point when the final decision is taken.

CONSISTENCY AND CREDIBILITY

Your CV may paint a glowing picture of you and your suitability for the job for which you are applying, but it won't do you much good if no one believes it.

⟨⟩ COACHING SESSION 51

The importance of consistency

Put yourself in the position of an employer faced with the task of interviewing candidates for a senior management appointment. One of the candidates hasn't been in his current job for very long and in his CV he has given his reason for wishing to leave as 'broken promises'. However, when the question 'Why are you looking for another job?' is put to him at the interview, he answers by referring to disputes with the CEO over the direction the business should be taking.

What would be your thoughts on this candidate? Record them here.

_____

_____

_____

_____

_____

_____

_____

_____

_____

_____

Minor inconsistencies such as these can serve to introduce an area of doubt where one may not have existed otherwise. While there is nothing to stop an interviewer seeking to clear up the doubt by asking the candidate to explain something in greater detail, many interviewers don't. A warning bell sounds somewhere inside their head and they go no further. All this goes to show that the issue of whether a candidate is telling the truth or not is a big one at interviews.

Avoid sowing seeds of doubt by making sure that any information you give in your CV marries up with information you give elsewhere. Pay particular attention to what you say in:

- your cover letter
- any online applications you make
- any application forms you fill in
- any information you give to intermediaries such as recruitment consultants
- any statements you make at interviews.

With regard to the last of these bullet points, consistency becomes harder to achieve as the selection process moves on. Here, what you say about yourself at one interview and what you say about yourself at the next also needs to be consistent.

The answer, of course, is to revisit your CV every time you go for an interview. Minor slip-ups that can serve to undermine your credibility are avoidable by making it a golden rule that you revisit the CV that you submitted in support of your job application *before* you go for an interview.

Remind yourself exactly what you said and do the same if you are asked at any point to complete an application form.

Remember, too, that, when you go for an interview, the interviewer will often have your CV and application form on the desk in front of them. They will therefore be able to see at a glance whether there are any discrepancies between what you say in your answers to their questions and what you have said about yourself elsewhere.

 COACH'S TIP

Keep copies

Another golden rule is always to keep a copy of any CV that you submit to an employer because, if you don't, you won't have anything to look back at when you're asked either to fill in an application form or to go to an interview.

Here are three last tips regarding your CV during the interview process:

1. **Keep a dossier on every job application** you make – that is, have a place where you file away documents such as the ad for the job, any correspondence you have had with the employer and, more importantly, a copy of the CV you sent in. You will find that it makes life much easier when the need arises to look back over everything.

2. **Print off a hard copy of any CV you submit**. PCs have an unfortunate habit of going wrong just at the moment you need them the most – for example, an hour before you're due to set off for an interview when you wanted to get your CV up on screen to refresh your memory. Print out the CV sent out to an employer so that you can file it away in your dossier and access it quickly and easily and without any bother.

3. **Take a copy of your CV with you** to an interview (the one you submitted when you applied for the job). This is because, when you arrive for an interview, you may well be given an application form to fill in. Without your CV to hand, you would find yourself not just scratching your head over dates but also trying to remember what you said about yourself.

NEXT STEPS

A CV isn't just there to get you interviews, and this chapter has demonstrated how the CV you have put some effort into preparing will go on working for you in the following ways:

- It will set the agenda for your interviews.

- It will direct attention to your best points.

- It will put you on course for getting the job.

Also in this chapter, you have seen how easy it is to put dents in your credibility by introducing inconsistencies into the information you present to employers. Consistency and credibility are inextricably linked and the answer here is to take care that everything you say about yourself in your CV, during the course of your interviews and in any other documentation you are asked to complete, marries up. Look at your CV again before you attend an interview, so that the information in it is fresh in your mind. You will find that this is time well spent.

The next chapter looks at how to measure the effectiveness of your CVs and how to make the judgement call on:

- whether your CVs are working for you or not

- when it may be time to make some changes.

TAKEAWAYS

As a result of reading this chapter, will you be changing the way you approach interviews? If so, what will you be doing differently?

_____

_____

_____

_____

_____

_____

_____

_____

_____

Have you changed your opinion about what a CV is there to do for you? If you have, then say in what way your opinion has changed.

_____

_____

_____

_____

_____

_____

_____

_____

_____

_____

_____

As a result of reading this chapter, will be you paying more attention in future to making sure that all the information you present to employers marries up? How do you plan to do this?

_____

_____

_____

_____

_____

_____

_____

_____

Is there any information about you that can be accessed by using the Internet – for example information on social networking sites? Is the information consistent with what you have said about yourself in your CV? If not, what do you plan to do about it?

_____

_____

_____

_____

_____

_____

_____

_____

_____

Did you take on board the advice about revisiting your CV before you go for an interview? Did you find this advice helpful? Is it something you will be doing the next time you're invited to attend an interview?

_____

_____

_____

_____

_____

_____

_____

_____

What in your opinion is the most useful advice in this chapter? Why did you find it useful?

_____

_____

_____

_____

_____

_____

_____

_____

_____

_____

CV MANAGEMENT

✔ OUTCOMES FROM THIS CHAPTER

- Understand how to measure your CV's performance.
- Know when it may be time to make a few changes.
- Know when it may be best to leave it alone.
- Understand why it's important to keep your CV updated.

🗩🗩 COACHING SESSION 52

Time for a change?

Consider the following statement. It comes from a male job seeker who has been active on the market for the last 18 months.

'I have lost count of the number of positions I have applied for (it must be around 30), but so far I haven't had much luck. In all, I have been invited to attend five interviews but up to now none of them has resulted in an offer of employment. Is this a signal to me that my CVs aren't working? In which case, has the time come to look at my CVs again with a view to giving them an overhaul?'

Put yourself in the position of someone who is advising this candidate and answer the question he has asked in the light of the information he has provided.

_____

_____

_____

_____

_____

MEASURING THE EFFECTIVENESS OF A CV

When there is tangible evidence that your CVs aren't working for you, then the right course of action is to go back to the drawing board and try a fresh approach. However, what to you may look like a poor return for all the effort that has gone into your job applications may not be the fault of your CVs – in which case, rehashing them won't be the answer and will be an unnecessary waste of your time.

Worse still, you could be scrapping perfectly acceptable CVs and replacing them with something inferior.

COACH'S TIP

Warning!

In the business of CV management, change isn't always for the better.

The job seeker in Coaching session 52 is a good example of someone who is at the receiving end of confused messages. Thirty applications, five interviews, no jobs – is this good or is it bad? Like most readings of performance connected with job seeking, the answer is not as straightforward as it seems. For a start – and before passing judgement – you would need to know more about him and the kind of jobs for which he is applying. For instance, he could be applying for a very narrow range of top jobs where the competition he will be up against will be formidable. In this case, five interviews from 30 applications could be seen as good going and evidence that his CV *is* working. Whether his interview skills could do with a brush-up is an entirely different matter, of course.

The classic test of how a CV has performed is to see whether it succeeded in getting you an interview or not. However, there are many reasons why applicants fail to get interviews, so, before jumping to the conclusion that your CV is to blame, run through the following checklist to see if there could be another explanation for your lack of success:

- **Are you overreaching?** Are you applying for jobs where you don't have all the qualifications and/or experience needed? While there is nothing wrong with setting your sights high, take on board that your chances of getting on the interview list are, at best, slight.

- **Are you applying for jobs that are beneath you?** A good example is the former senior manager who has been out of work for some time and starts applying for 'anything and everything' in an effort to keep the wolf from the door. Again, there is nothing wrong with lowering your expectations if you should ever find yourself in the unenviable position of needing a job just to make ends meet but, at the same time, you should be aware that people applying for jobs way beneath their capabilities are, on the whole, viewed with suspicion by employers. Not without good reason, employers feel that such people are (a) only looking for a port in a storm and (b) will move on as soon as they can find something better (something more in line with their capabilities).

- **Are your applications long shots?** Are you looking to achieve something intrinsically difficult such as change your career? If so, getting on the interview list is going to be tough and you shouldn't expect it to be any different.

- **Are you in a disadvantaged group?** In job market terms, someone who is disadvantaged is someone who doesn't have a full set of skills and qualifications (in many cases owing to lack of opportunity). Getting interviews is always going to be an uphill struggle if you belong to a disadvantaged group.

- **Are you there to take the calls?** This is a reminder that lack of success on the job market is often down to basics. As you saw earlier in the book, many interviews are arranged over the phone, so people who are hard to contact can be passed over just for that reason.

- **Are you focusing too much attention on jobs that have been advertised?** The advertised or visible job market is where you will come up against most competition and where, as a consequence, your chances of getting on the interview list are slimmest. The answer here is to introduce more balance into your job-seeking by seeing what opportunities the invisible market may have to offer, rather than embarking on a radical overhaul of your CV.

 **COACH'S TIP**

It's not always the CV!

When you get turned down for a job, don't automatically assume that your CV is at fault.

The number of interviews you get tells you little about how your CVs are performing. For example, what if the interviews are for jobs that turn out to be unsuitable? What if you find that you achieve nothing apart from notching up a few bad experiences and wasting your time? What would, of course, be an entirely different matter is if the interviews you sourced were for jobs that came up to your expectations. Then perhaps you could say that your CVs had performed well.

COACHING SESSION 53

Over to you

What measures would you apply to form a judgement on whether your CVs are working for you or not?

Write your thoughts down here.

_____

_____

_____

_____

_____

_____

_____

_____

_____

WHEN THE TIME COMES TO MAKE CHANGES

There are so many factors in play when it comes to making job applications that it's practically impossible to say whether any one of them (or a combination of several) provides the explanation for why you don't seem to be having much joy. It could be your CV that's at fault, or, there again, it could be the sourcing methods you're using or the nature of the market you're attacking.

However, if your applications keep drawing a blank, sooner or later the time comes to take stock. Here 'taking stock' means reviewing your entire strategy, not just your CV. When should you do it? There are no set time intervals and, to a large extent, it depends on how many job applications you are making. But say, for example, that you send off 20 applications and you don't get invited to a single interview. This could be a signal to take a good, hard look at what you're doing, including having another crack at putting together the framework of your CV.

COACH'S TIP

Warning!

Changing your approach in response to negative events, such as every time you receive a turn-down letter, isn't a good way to proceed. Your approach will lack continuity and it will be difficult to make any kind of assessment of whether it is working for you or not.

One of the great twenty-first century myths regarding CVs is that there is an ideal model out there somewhere that beats all-comers. Belief in the myth of the perfect CV is the main cause of people spending hours in front of a screen constantly striving for something better. What happens is this: people apply for jobs and then, when they don't seem to be having much success, start making minor changes to their CVs. Yes, it may seem harmless enough, but, apart from being largely wasted effort, it introduces the difficulty of never being able to accumulate enough evidence to assess whether a particular approach to the design of your CV works for you or not.

There is no such thing as the perfect CV, so put this idea out of your head. CVs are about people and what's good about people is their diversity. Yes, your CV has to perform a task for you but, providing you follow the ground rules set out in the earlier chapters of this book, there is still a lot of scope for you to inject a little of your own personality into the design of your CVs.

Remember the point in Chapter 1 about standard templates of the kind you find in books or you can download off the Internet? They're bland. They all look the same and, to someone who has been given the job of reading a batch of CVs, the experience can be mind-numbing. So, without going over the top, don't be afraid to experiment with the design of your CVs. If you don't seem to be having much luck with your job applications, try ringing the changes every now and then.

UPDATING THE INFORMATION IN YOUR CV

Keeping the framework version of your CV up to date is all part of good CV management. Do you already have a framework version of your CV? If so, when was it last updated?

Unless you happen to be currently active on the job market, it's a safe bet that the most recent version of your CV is one that you put together some time ago. In the intervening period, you may have had no need for a CV, but then what happens when the pay rise you expected doesn't materialize or you're passed over for promotion or, worse still, you find that your name is on a redundancy list? What then? You will need to get some irons in the fire urgently. You will need to put out feelers, send off job applications, start talking to consultants and so on. And to do any of these things you will need an up-to-date CV.

COACHING SESSION 54

Review your last CV

Get out a copy of the last CV you put together and pick out any information in it that is either out of date or no longer relevant.

Make a list of what you find here.

_____
_____
_____
_____
_____
_____
_____
_____
_____

If you find yourself in the situation of needing a CV in a hurry and you have done nothing about keeping the framework version up to date, then the temptation will be to succumb to the pressure you're under and dash one off quickly. Whether the result will be consistent with your best efforts or not will be a matter for you and your conscience, but the message here is this. In an uncertain world, where you never know what is round the next corner, it pays to be poised, which means not having to dig out from the back of drawers the information you need to bring your CV up to date. Having the framework version already in a form that only calls for a few finishing touches will allow you to focus your undivided attention on the finer points.

NEXT STEPS

This chapter has been about CV management and in what circumstances making changes to your CV is and isn't desirable. On the one hand, it is important to keep the framework version of your CV up to date so that it is ready to be used if the need should arise. On the other, there are dangers in endlessly revising CVs. This is because:

- it can become obsessive

- it can serve to distract you from forming a proper and more rounded view of how your CVs are performing.

The next chapter looks at the subject of cover letters. A great CV needs a great cover letter to go with it and one without the other doesn't work. It is important, therefore, that you put just as much effort into your cover letters as you do into your CVs. What's more, your cover letters and CVs need to look as if they've been written by the same person; otherwise they will attract negative attention. This is the challenge that Chapter 10 will seek to address.

TAKEAWAYS

Has reading this chapter made you think again about how to measure the performance of your CVs? In what way has your thinking changed?

_____

_____

_____

_____

_____

_____

_____

_____

_____

Did you find the advice in this chapter about not reacting to negative events useful? How will this advice help you when you next have to deal with the disappointment of being turned down for a job?

_____

_____

_____

_____

_____

_____

_____

_____

_____

_____

Has the point about not basing your judgements on how many interviews you get made you think again? Will you be adopting a different measure of success in future and, if so, what measure will you use?

_____

_____

_____

_____

_____

_____

_____

_____

_____

Has reading this chapter prompted you to bring the framework version of your CV up to date? What steps will you take and what deadline will you set for doing this?

_____

_____

_____

_____

_____

_____

_____

_____

_____

_____

In terms of looking at reasons for not getting interviews, did you find the checklist in this chapter helpful? In the past, have you tended to pin the blame for lack of success on the design of your CV? If so, was there anything in the checklist that caused you to think you could be barking up the wrong tree?

_____

_____

_____

_____

_____

_____

_____

_____

_____

As a result of reading this chapter, will you be more inclined to think twice before making changes to your CV?

_____

_____

_____

_____

_____

_____

_____

_____

_____

_____

10 COVER LETTERS

✔ OUTCOMES FROM THIS CHAPTER

- Understand the important part that cover letters play in moving job applications to successful conclusions.
- Know how to put together a good cover letter.
- Recognize how your cover letter is an integral part of your CV.

A CV isn't a stand-alone item. If it's being sent to someone (e.g. an employer), it needs a cover letter to go with it.

🗩🗩 COACHING SESSION 55

Penny Pritchard's cover letter

Below is an example of a cover letter. What in your opinion is wrong with it? Give your answer here.

_____

_____

_____

_____

_____

_____

_____

Penny Pritchard
10 North Street
Twiddleton-on-Tweed
TW99 9XX
Tel: xxxxxxxx
Mobile: xxxxx xxxxxx
Email: pennyp@xxx.com

30 March 2014

Sally Simpson
Human Resources Manager
Doggy Dins Pet Foods Limited
Willow Tree Industrial Estate
Twiddleton on Tweed
TW77 7DD

Dear Sally Simpson,

Re: Area Sales Manager (ref – SS/01/02)

I wish to apply for the above position advertised in last night's *Evening Bugle.*

A copy of my CV is enclosed.

I am available for interview at any time and look forward to hearing from you.
Yours sincerely,

Penny Pritchard

Penny Pritchard
Enc.: CV

THE ROLE COVER LETTERS PLAY

Cover letters occupy a unique place because they are what employers read first. More to the point, how they are received plays a crucial role in determining what happens next. For example, a cover letter that arrives written on a scruffy piece of paper and full of spelling mistakes stands a good chance of being fed into the shredding machine along with the CV that came with it. Even if the CV does get a reading, the cover letter will have left a mark in the employer's mind that won't be easy to eradicate. As you saw earlier in the book, first impressions, good or bad, have a tendency to stick.

 COACH'S TIP

Send the right signal with your cover letter

Sad to say, a common feature of cover letters is that, compared with CVs, they don't have the same level of care lavished on them. The result in a lot of cases is a cover letter and a CV that appear to have been written by different people and this, to an employer, can send out an unfortunate signal.

What did you find wrong with the cover letter Penny Pritchard put together to go with her application to Doggy Dins Pet Foods in Coaching session 55? And what did you think were the good points?

Among the good points about Penny's letter are that it is concise and well set out. The grammar is fine and there are no spelling mistakes. In fact, Penny comes across as someone who goes straight to the point and who is businesslike – qualities that would seemingly make her a good candidate for a management position in sales.

So where has she gone wrong? A cover letter is another place where you can draw attention to your strong points, but Penny doesn't do this. In fact, she says nothing about herself and this is a pity. In short, she has missed an opportunity to score a few important points at a stage in the selection process where it matters most – *at the beginning*.

 COACH'S TIP

Warning!

There are still people out there who feel they can dispense with cover letters. They send in CVs attached to business cards or home-made compliments slips. Alternatively, the cover letters they write consist of two sentences along the lines of 'I wish to apply for the position of [...]. A copy of my CV is enclosed. Yours sincerely.'

WHAT TO PUT IN A COVER LETTER

The test of a good cover letter is whether or not it prompts the reader to find out more. 'More' in this case means that the reader is led to look at your CV. In other words, your cover letter is there to whet the reader's appetite.

COACHING SESSION 56

Whet the reader's appetite

Based on what you have learned so far in this book, what in your view would encourage a recipient of your CV to want to find out more about you?

Write your answer here.

_____

_____

_____

_____

_____

_____

_____

_____

_____

_____

_____

_____

_____

_____

_____

_____

Employers who read cover letters aren't such hard nuts to crack as some authorities make out. Yes, they are busy people with all sorts of conflicting demands on their time, but they are also people who are trying to fill vacant slots and, in some cases, these vacant slots may be causing them difficulties. Take, for example, the CEO of a large logistics operation whose Head of Finance has just walked out a few weeks ahead of the time of year when budgets and profit forecasts need to be prepared for the Board. Someone who ticks all the boxes will be manna from heaven as far as this CEO is concerned! So, in short, what your cover letter needs to demonstrate is that you are someone who ticks all the boxes.

This takes you back into familiar territory – the front page of your CV and the key matches between these two things:

- the requirements of the job
- what you have to offer.

So is it a case of putting in your cover letter the same list of bullet points that appears in the key skills and achievements section of your CV? Almost, although in the interests of concision it may be better to pick out what you see as the most important of your bullet points and summarize each in a couple of simple sentences.

COACHING SESSION 57

John Everyman's cover letter

Here is another example of a cover letter. Compare this cover letter with the one in Coaching session 55.

Write down here what you see as the main differences.

_____

_____

_____

_____

_____

_____

_____

_____

_____

John Everyman

12 Acacia Gardens

Any town AT99 9XX

Tel: xxx xxxxx

Mobile: xxx xxxxxx

Email:– Johne@xxx.com

29 March 2014

Julie Robertson

Human Resources Manager

XX Extruded Sections Limited

PO Box xx

Anytown

AT11 1ZZ

Dear Julie Robertson,

Re: Factory Manager

I wish to apply for the position advertised in last night's *Evening Bugle.* You will see from my CV (attached) that I am currently employed as a Cell Manager in a precision engineering company where I am responsible for 120 operatives working four on/four off continental shifts. I am aware of XX Extruded Sections' excellent reputation and I would welcome the opportunity to talk further about joining your management team.

With regard to the requirements set out in your advertisement:

- **Modern manufacturing techniques** Information on the training I have received is given in my CV. In my present job I have been closely involved with the introduction of fast tooling changes.

- **Qualifications** I have a degree in Mechanical Engineering.

- **Management experience** I have been in my present position for five years and previously worked for eight years as a Shift Manager in charge of a high-volume production unit.

- **Additional information** For five years post-apprenticeship I worked on the design of a range of dies and tools including plastic and aluminium extrusion dies.

Apart from Monday morning when I chair production meetings, I am available for interview at any time. My current employment is subject to one calendar month's notice.

I look forward to hearing from you.

Yours sincerely

John Everyman

John Everyman

Attached: CV

Careers advisors often flag up the need to keep cover letters to one side of A4. The thinking here is that one side of A4 will act as a constraint on writers of cover letters, so they don't end up with pages of script that no one will ever bother to read. However, you may find it hard to fit everything you want to say about yourself into the available space. If this is the case, it is fine to go to two pages.

COACH'S TIP

The one-side 'rule'

A cover letter that conforms to the rule of one side of A4 won't do much for you if it doesn't say anything about you that is relevant to the job for which you're applying. Similarly, a cover letter that is full of relevant information but which rambles on for page after page won't do the trick for you either.

Don't therefore:

- sacrifice important messages for no other reason than they won't fit on to one page

- try to resolve the problem by, for example, reducing the width of your page margins or cutting down on the size of your font or anything else that will make your letter uninviting to read.

WRITING A COVER LETTER

With the advent of email, people don't get called on to write business letters in the same way that they used to 20 or 30 years ago, so, to some extent, business letter writing has become a lost art. Perhaps it is not surprising therefore that a large segment of the population find it challenging when they are put in the position of having to write a cover letter that has to go in the post.

Forms of salutation

COACHING SESSION 58

A short test

Imagine you have seen an advertisement for a job where applicants are invited to put a CV in the post to Gillian Fishbourne, Human Resources Manager. At the start of your letter how do you address Gillian Fishbourne?

Put a tick in the box alongside the form of salutation you would choose:

Dear Madam ☐

Dear Ms Fishbourne ☐

Dear Mrs Fishbourne ☐

Dear Miss Fishbourne ☐

Dear Gillian ☐

Dear Gillian Fishbourne ☐

So what is the right way to address Gillian Fishbourne? After all, you don't know her and 'Dear Gillian' could be seen as being a bit over-familiar. To complicate matters further, you don't know whether she's a Miss, Mrs or Ms. 'Dear Madam' puts you on safer ground but it could hardly be described as engaging. There is also evidence to suggest that someone addressed by name is more likely to reply to you. This leaves 'Dear Gillian Fishbourne', which is professional and formal without being starchy yet, at the same time, personal and direct.

Writing to a man doesn't quite have the same complications as writing to a woman so, if you're invited to send your application to Tim Shaw, you can address him as 'Dear Tim Shaw' or 'Dear Mr Shaw' – either is acceptable. 'Dear Tim Shaw' probably has the edge because including his first name is more engaging.

COACHING SESSION 59

Another short test

What if the advertisement doesn't give a name and asks you to write to the Human Resources Manager? You don't know whether the Human Resources Manager is a man or a woman, so does this leave you with no choice other than to begin your letter with 'Dear Sir or Madam'.

Write your answer here.

_____

_____

When you have no other information on the person to whom you are writing apart from a job title, there is nothing wrong with starting the letter with 'Dear Sir or Madam' except that it's not very engaging. One approach you might like to consider is writing to 'Dear Human Resources Manager'. It's different and engages with the person more than a starchy 'Dear Sir or Madam'. At least you're addressing them with their job title, which is perhaps the next best thing to their name.

! COACH'S TIP

Spell the addressee's name correctly

Be careful when you're typing in people's names and make sure you copy them correctly. Mistakes are more common than you may think and, not surprisingly, the person whose name you've spelled wrongly will notice it straight away. How they view your failure to get their name right will be a matter for them, but what it doesn't say a lot for is your attention to detail.

Make it clear why you're writing

This is important. Organizations often have more than one position that they are advertising, so, to avoid your letter and CV being put in the wrong pile of applications, make it clear which job interests you. The example cover letters in Coaching sessions 55 and 57 show how you can achieve this by putting a heading at the top of your letter. In one case, the candidate has been asked to quote a reference – which she has done. Where you see vacancies referenced in this way, always follow the instructions.

Your opening paragraph

The opening paragraph of your cover letter needs to make it clear why you are applying for the job. As you saw earlier in the book, employers need to know:

- where you're coming from
- what you're seeking to achieve.

◖◖ COACHING SESSION 60

Example

Here is an example of an opening paragraph:

'I wish to apply for the position of Logistics Manager advertised in last night's *Evening Bugle*. A copy of my CV is attached from which you will see that I am currently employed as a Logistics Manager in a national freight haulage business. I am seeking a new position because the hub where I am based is due for closure in six months' time, at which point I will be made redundant.'

Do you have any comment about what this candidate has had to say about why he's applying for the job? Write your answer here.

_____

_____

_____

_____

_____

_____

In today's world of work, being at risk of redundancy is a common enough reason for needing to find another job, but, on its own, it can convey the impression that the candidate is desperate and anything will do to get them out of a tight corner. It can even convey the impression that the candidate has no great interest in the job and only applied for it because of the situation they find themselves in. Sadly, employers have had their fingers burned with people who take on jobs just to avoid being out of work, only to leave again as soon as they find something better.

COACH'S TIP

Be positive

Even if you are in a redundancy situation, always have something positive to say about why you're applying for the job – for example, you want to come and work for the business because of its reputation or the position advertised fits exactly with where you see yourself next (or both). Adding a sentence along these lines could make all the difference if, at the final stage in selection, you're neck and neck with another candidate and where the decision could rest on who really wants the job most.

The cover letter in Coaching session 57 contains a good example of an opening paragraph that makes it clear why the candidate (John Everyman) wants the job.

Your strong points

After your opening paragraph is where your list of bulleted strong points comes in. Remember that what you're seeking to achieve is to capture the reader's interest to such an extent that he or she will to want to look at your CV.

Closing paragraph

All you have to do now is tell the employer that your CV is enclosed and at the same time say a few words about:

- when you can attend interviews
- when you would be available to start a new job.

ONLINE RESOURCE

What to say about your availability

Download a list of these dos and don'ts on what to say about your availability in the closing paragraph of a cover letter.

Don't say you're only available for interviews after 6 p.m. or on Saturday mornings. If you do, you won't find too many takers.

Do try to give employers as much leeway as you can with interview times.

Don't say you're available when you're not.

Do give details of any holidays, dates when you can't attend, etc.

Don't leave unanswered questions. For example, if your branch is closing in six months' time does it mean you can't start a job for six months?

Do see it from the employer's point of view. If you are on a redundancy list and the date you've been given is still some way off, tell the employer what the position would be if they offered you a job. For example, are any arrangements in place for early release?

Don't (if you're employed) make statements like 'I could start a new job at any time', which gives the impression that you would leave your current position without giving the proper notice. Understandably, employers don't warm to people who are prepared to act in this way – i.e. it's a bad first impression.

Do state the period of notice set out in your terms of employment.

Go to the following website:

www.TYCoachbooks.com/CVs

Signing off

All that remains is to finish your letter by signing off at the end in the proper way.

 COACHING SESSION 61

How should you sign off?

Do you have any views on how best to sign off a cover letter? Would you end it 'Yours faithfully' or 'Yours sincerely', or in some other way?

Write your answer down here.

_____

_____

_____

_____

_____

_____

_____

_____

There are only two acceptable ways of ending a business letter – one is 'Yours sincerely' and the other is 'Yours faithfully'. So forget 'Best wishes' or 'Kind regards' or anything else you may put at the end of a letter to someone with whom you have had correspondence before. 'Yours sincerely' should be used if you started the letter with someone's name (e.g. 'Dear Gillian Fishbourne'). Use 'Yours faithfully' if the letter started with 'Dear Sir' or 'Dear Madam'.

! COACH'S TIP

Follow the etiquette

Don't run away with the idea that employers don't care any more about the etiquette of business letters. They do. What's more, the cover letter you put with your CV when you apply for a job gives them a good opportunity to see what you're capable of doing.

🗪🗪 COACHING SESSION 62

No signature?

Put yourself in an employer's position. How would you react if you received a cover letter that hadn't been signed? What might it suggest to you?

Write your answer here.

_____

_____

_____

_____

_____

_____

❗ COACH'S TIP

Warning!

A cover letter that isn't signed could suggest lack of attention to detail on the part of whoever submitted it – a bad point of the kind that employers can and do pick up on. However, some employers take a much harsher view, seeing a cover letter that doesn't bear a signature as possible evidence that the information in it isn't true.

After 'Yours sincerely' or 'Yours faithfully', leave five line spaces for your signature, then type in your name – your first name and your surname. Writing 'J. Brown' or, worse still, 'Miss J. Brown', looks old-fashioned and standoffish when the general idea is to engage with the reader.

What else?

Insert another line space after your name, then type in 'Attached: CV'. This is a way of bringing your cover letter and CV together. When you have done this, staple your cover letter to your CV to reduce the risk of them becoming separated when they're taken out of the envelope at the other end.

HANDWRITTEN COVER LETTERS

If you're putting a cover letter in the post (as opposed to submitting it by email), you have the choice of handwriting it. Your handwriting needs to be neat and legible, of course, but is there any objection to doing this?

Thanks to modern technology, you can compose your cover letter on screen, spell-check it, edit it if it's too long, alter it if you change your mind about anything and run off drafts as and when you please. You don't have the same flexibility with a pen-and-ink cover letter, meaning that, if you made a mistake, you would probably be left with no choice other than to start all over again.

COACHING SESSION 63

To type or handwrite?

Some people prefer to handwrite their cover letters because they think it gives them an extra bit of style and individuality. Do you have a view on handwritten cover letters? What do you see as the advantages and disadvantages?

Advantages

_____

_____

_____

_____

_____

_____

Disadvantages

_____

_____

_____

_____

_____

COACH'S TIP

Keep a copy

Always run off a hard copy of anything you send to an employer, including your cover letter. Keep the copy with everything else to do with your application (i.e. in a separate folder). You will remember from Chapter 8 how important it is to revisit your CV and cover letter every time you go for an interview. You therefore need a copy of your cover letter that you can get your hands on quickly.

At the same time, always save your cover letters in the documents you store on your PC. Don't do as some people do and overwrite them in the mistaken belief that they have no further use after they've been printed off and put in the post.

SUBMITTING A COVER LETTER BY EMAIL

Many job ads ask you to submit your CV by email. Email scores highly in terms of the speed and certainty of its arrival at its destination. Furthermore, if the ad invited you to send the email to a named individual, it's a safe bet that he/she will open it and read it straight away.

COACHING SESSION 64

A potential problem

The normal way of submitting an application by email is to put your cover letter in the body of the email and your CV in a file attachment. Do you see any problem with this? If so, what is the problem and what ways can you suggest of getting round it?

Write your answer here.

_____

_____

_____

_____

_____

_____

What happens in many cases is that when your email is received at the other end, the file attachment containing your CV is printed off whereas the email itself isn't. As a result, all the effort that went into your cover letter is wasted. It may not even be read.

To avoid this situation, put a copy of your cover letter in the file attachment, so that it effectively becomes the first page of your CV (more on this below).

The issue of file attachments that don't open was dealt with in Chapter 3. Remember therefore to carry out the test of sending an email with a blank file attachment to someone you know rather than leaving it to chance.

STANDARDS OF ENGLISH IN EMAILS

Email has brought a new dimension to the problem of people's spelling and word usage thanks to a widely held view that corresponding with someone by email doesn't call for the same levels of care and attention. Similarly, there is a view in some circles that it is acceptable to dispense with the usual forms of salutation and signing off and to replace them with 'Hi' and 'Cheers' and the like.

As a job application progresses through its various stages, you will, if all goes well, be receiving emails from the employer inviting you to attend interviews and second interviews and eventually an email offering you the job. In these emails, you could find that the employer starts and ends them with 'Hi' and 'Cheers' or something similar which is on the whole an encouraging sign and an invitation to you to respond in a like manner. In fact, to do otherwise could be seen as stiff and standoffish. However, to begin with, it is safer by far to stick to conventional forms of salutation and signing off. In other words, the text of your email should be no different from the text of a cover letter you are putting in the post.

COACH'S TIP

Remember...

Don't forget the warning earlier in the book that it's a bad idea to send in unsolicited CVs by email.

BRING YOUR COVER LETTER AND CV TOGETHER

As already mentioned, a cover letter should be seen as an integral part of your CV. Together they are a team. Apart, they have no meaning.

The purpose of a cover letter is to bring out the key points in your application. In effect, you're saying to your reader, 'Here's what's good about me and, if it interests you and you want to find out more, take a look at my CV.' Put another way, your cover letter serves as an appetizer to the main course – your CV.

It is important therefore to bring your cover letter and CV together physically:

■ Staple one to the other when you put them in the post.

■ When you're sending an application by email, put a copy of your cover letter in the file attachment containing your CV.

Ensuring as far as you can that your cover letter and CV stay together will help you to steer your application to a successful conclusion. As the selection process unfolds, they will pass from one person to the next and in this way they will go on working for you right through to the point at which the final decision is taken. Remember that, in a close-run race between two equally well-qualified candidates, someone who has taken the time and trouble to put together a good cover letter may be seen as better than someone who hasn't. They showed a bit more interest, and, to employers, this matters.

 COACH'S TIP

Give your cover letter the attention it needs

Even today, when most job seekers are clued up about what to do and have a lot of expert advice available to them, the cover letter is still the poor relation when it comes to presenting employers with a set of credentials that will impress them. Cover letters continue to come in that show little evidence of having the same care and attention lavished on them as the CVs that accompany them. So, attach proper importance to the job of putting together a good cover letter and take advantage of the fact that many people who try hard in other directions neglect to do the same.

NEXT STEPS

This chapter has been about making sure that any CV you produce has a good cover letter to go with it. A cover letter is what an employer reads first and, if they see something that interests them, they will read the CV that accompanies it. Conversely, if the cover letter says nothing, there will be nothing to spur them on to enquire further. The CV may get a glance through or it may not, depending on how many other applications have been received. In this way, many perfectly well-qualified candidates end up selling themselves short.

The final chapter of the book brings together some of the lessons from previous chapters. What it also sets out to demonstrate is that you can get better at writing CVs. Because so much in today's world of work hangs on the ability to produce winning CVs, the benefits for you are enormous, both in terms of the opportunities you will be able to access and in the development of your career.

TAKEAWAYS

Is there anything new you have learned about the part that cover letters play? List the key points here.

_____

_____

_____

_____

_____

_____

_____

_____

_____

_____

_____

_____

_____

_____

_____

As a result of reading this chapter, do you think you could benefit from paying greater attention to the design of your cover letters? Where do you think your effort would be best placed?

_____

_____

_____

_____

_____

_____

_____

_____

_____

_____

_____

_____

_____

_____

Did you find the point about bringing your cover letter and CV together in one document useful? Is it something that you intend to do in future?

_____

_____

_____

_____

_____

_____

_____

_____

_____

_____

_____

_____

_____

_____

_____

Have you learned anything new about what needs to go in a cover letter? As a result of reading this chapter, what information will you be putting in your cover letters that you haven't done previously?

_____

_____

_____

_____

_____

_____

_____

_____

_____

_____

_____

_____

Conversely, what information (if any) will you be leaving out? Say why you feel this information is no longer relevant.

_____

_____

_____

_____

_____

_____

_____

_____

_____

_____

_____

_____

_____

Did the online checklist help you to highlight any areas where you could be going wrong with the design of your cover letters? What did you pick out?

_____

_____

_____

_____

_____

_____

_____

_____

_____

_____

_____

_____

_____

ONLINE RESOURCE

Cover letter checklist

Go through the checklist and put a tick against the questions to which you can truthfully answer 'yes'.

- Are your cover letters typed on one sheet of plain white A4 paper? ☐
- Do you design a new cover letter every time you apply for a job? ☐
- Other than using a spellchecker, do you check your spelling and grammar rigorously? ☐
- Are you identifying your strong points? ☐
- Are your strong points matched to the skills, experience and qualifications the employer is seeking? ☐
- Is everything in your cover letters capable of being understood in one quick read? ☐
- Do you check for consistency between the information in your cover letters and what appears in your CV? ☐
- Do you always remember to sign your cover letters? ☐
- Have you done background research into employers and taken the trouble to find out more about them? ☐
- Are you getting your applications in the post promptly? ☐
- With emails, are you including a copy of your cover letter in the file attachment with your CV? ☐
- Are you making it clear to employers what interests you about working for them? ☐

Download this checklist to help you highlight any areas where you may be going wrong with your cover letters. Go to the following website:

www.TYCoachbooks.com/CVs

11 | MOVING INTO THE FUTURE

OUTCOMES FROM THIS CHAPTER

- Know how you can perfect the art of writing CVs.
- Understand how practice helps.
- Recognize what you can learn from the experience.

PERFECT THE ART OF WRITING A GOOD CV

◗◗ COACHING SESSION 65

The art of the précis

Take an article from a newspaper or a magazine or a chapter of a book and précis it into a few short paragraphs. When you have finished, go over what you have done and see if you can précis it any further.

Writing a good CV (and a good cover letter) is an exercise in saying all you need to say about yourself:

- clearly
- in as few words as possible.

The ability to write clearly and concisely is not a gift that comes overnight, so, rather than try to get it right first time, a useful way to proceed is to prepare your CV in draft, then see what you can do to précis it without going too far and taking out information that will make it less effective in terms of performing the task you want it to perform. In the fullness of time, you will find that you don't have to do this. Writing clearly and concisely will come naturally to you and you will see the benefits in other ways – not just in turning out good CVs and cover letters.

COACH'S TIP

Writing a précis is great exercise for...

- increasing your vocabulary
- improving your grammar and spelling
- expressing yourself clearly and concisely
- making you think
- putting together a CV.

COACHING SESSION 66

A bad impression

Put yourself in the shoes of an employer. How would it matter to you if a CV and cover letter came in poorly written and full of bad grammar and spelling mistakes? What impression would you form of the person who had produced them?

Jot down your thoughts here.

_____

_____

_____

_____

_____

_____

_____

_____

Your CV is a reflection of you, so, for example, if it is messy and all over the place, that's the image of you that it transmits to whoever reads it. Similarly, if your CV is full of silly mistakes, it sends out a message that you're slipshod, careless and incapable of paying attention to detail.

Surprisingly, perhaps, there are a lot of people still out there who feel it doesn't matter if CVs and cover letters are poorly written and/or riddled with mistakes. So long as they make sense, why get hung up about the odd bad construction or apostrophe in the wrong place?

What won't have escaped anyone's attention is that, in today's world, more and more business is conducted in writing thanks to email and other online forms of communication. Less and less of what people do involves the use of the spoken word, either in face-to-face conversations or over the phone. As a consequence, employers are extra wary of hiring people who can't spell or whose writing skills are poor. Understandably, customers are put off when they see emails or information displayed on websites that are full of mistakes. They think twice about doing business with the organization in question.

 ONLINE RESOURCE

Poor English in job applications

A joke doing the rounds recently was that, if a job application came in that was well written, free from spelling mistakes and with all the apostrophes in the right place, it had to be from a foreigner.

It seems that hardly a week goes by without comments in the headlines about the poor standard of English in job applications, but nothing appears to change. This is surprising because English is central to everything we do and worth the effort it takes to get it right. With a job application, our aim should be to catch an employer's eye with our skills and abilities – not with our bad grammar and spelling mistakes.

However, contrary to popular belief, the culprits aren't always school dropouts or other unfortunates. They're not all young people, either. They are often seemingly well-educated, well-qualified individuals across all age groups who, in many cases, have been to top colleges and universities. Nevertheless, they are often just as capable of letting themselves down when it comes to writing coherent and grammatically correct sentences. Their applications don't get far but they never find out why; they go on submitting letters and CVs that send shudders down employers' spines.

Isn't it the responsibility of each one of us to make sure that anything we send along in support of a job application projects an image consistent with the one we want to communicate? No one wants to be seen as careless or the kind of person who doesn't have the capacity to pay attention to detail, but this is how an application riddled with mistakes comes across. The person who put it together couldn't be bothered to check it properly, which, to an employer, doesn't say a lot for how the same person might get on when given some real responsibilities.

To give you some idea of how serious the problem is, we can quote the example of an applicant who got the company's name wrong (all she had to do was copy it from the advertisement). Then there was the honours graduate who thought 'current' as in 'current employment' should be spelt 'currant' as in ingredients for a fruitcake.

It's not that hard, is it…?

Find these words on the subject of poor English in the free download. Visit the following website:

www.TYCoachbooks.com/CVs

COACHING SESSION 67

How good is your English?

How do you rate when it comes to grammar and spelling? Write down your ideas on how you would make sure that your CVs don't send shudders down the spines of employers who read them.

_____

_____

_____

_____

_____

_____

_____

Spellcheckers are useful aids but they do have one big drawback. They give people a false impression of how good they are when it comes to spelling words correctly. Just because what they've typed doesn't come up on screen with a red line under it, they think everything's fine when in many cases it isn't. They don't proofread; they don't get out the dictionary; they don't take the trouble to get a second opinion, and, as a result, they let themselves down badly. There is, however, an even bigger problem for people who are unaware of their own limitations. They carry on doing what they have always done. They keep submitting CVs that are full of mistakes, and, of course, no one ever explains to them why their job applications go nowhere.

TAKE OWNERSHIP OF YOUR CV

How you come across when your CV is subjected to the 'one quick read' test can be the difference between success and failure, especially when:

- you are one of many applicants for the job
- any CVs in which the grammar and spelling don't come up to scratch could automatically find their way on to the reject pile.

Thoughts such as these are part of taking ownership of your CV in the context of what you want it to deliver.

COACH'S TIP

It's carelessness, not ignorance

Most glaring errors found in CVs are the result of carelessness rather than the writer's knowledge of English letting them down. Carelessness is easily addressed.

What the experience of writing a CV teaches you

Writing a CV and doing it properly teaches you to express yourself clearly and concisely in writing, which is a skill that you can bring into other areas of your life. What's more, in an online age, the ability to write fluently and in a compact style is arguably more important than it has ever been.

There is a further point here and it is this. The quality of the image you project has important ramifications as far as the future of your career is concerned. If you project a good image, you get on and go places. If you don't, then the opposite tends to happen. How well you can write plays a big part in projecting the right image. Writing that is snappy and straight to the point is the outward manifestation of an organized and tidy mind. Writing that strays off the point and rambles all over the place suggests the exact opposite. Writing that is full of careless mistakes suggests someone who could cost a business money.

🗨🗨 COACHING SESSION 68

Gathering useful ideas

From time to time, your job may call on you to look at CVs that have come in – for example, CVs that have been received in response to an advertisement that your organization has placed. Here you will be viewing what's in front of you with a different pair of eyes and the experience is one you can learn from. As you go through the CVs and pick out those that interest you, try to make a point of asking yourself exactly what has caught your attention. No one has sole ownership of the right to produce really great CVs and you can learn much from the efforts of others. In some cases, you will see CVs that are very different in terms of their appearance but which do a good job just the same.

Use the space below to jot down any interesting ideas you come across (ideas you may want to incorporate into your own CVs).

_____

_____

_____

_____

_____

_____

_____

_____

_____

_____

_____

_____

_____

_____

_____

_____

_____

NEXT STEPS

Creating a great CV should be seen in the context of a continuous improvement process. You are always striving for the next one to be better than the last and this chapter has been about what you can do to perfect the art of writing CVs that will:

- project the image of you that you want to project

- do you justice

- achieve what you want them to achieve.

More CVs end up being fed into the shredding machine because of their poor standards of literacy than for any other reason, so much of the focus in this chapter has been on what you can do to avoid slip-ups such as silly spelling mistakes. Everyone is capable of making the odd gaffe here and there and one of the important lessons to learn as you sit down to the task of preparing a CV is to be aware of your own limitations.

You have now reached the end of the book and the point where it is now over to you to decide where you want to take what you have learned next.

TAKEAWAYS

Now that you have read this book, what is left for you to consider is:

- how much of what you have learned you have found useful
- what you will take away with you.

To help put your thoughts in order and, at the same time, act as a revision exercise, the following checklist summarizes the main messages in the book. Add your own thoughts about these messages to the spaces below.

1 A CV is there to perform the task you want it to perform. ☐

_____

_____

2 Design your CV to make it perform the task. ☐

_____

_____

3 Don't expect one CV to perform all the tasks. ☐

_____

_____

4 Make your CVs relevant to the task you want them to perform. ☐

_____

_____

5 Keep them concise. ☐

_____

_____

6 Pay attention to the quality of your English and, in particular, your spelling. ☐

_____

_____

7 Make it clear in your CVs where you're coming from and what you're seeking to achieve. ☐

_____

_____

8 Don't use your CVs to pull the wool over employers' eyes. ☐

_____

9 Always have an up-to-date framework version of your CV available. ☐

_____

10 Put some effort into designing a good front page. ☐

_____

11 Use your CVs to attack and overcome the competition. ☐

_____

12 Revisit your CV every time you go for an interview. ☐

_____

13 Don't do anything to put dents in your credibility. ☐

_____

14 Don't react to negative events. ☐

_____

15 Judge CVs on what counts. ☐

_____

16 A great CV needs a great cover letter to go with it. ☐

_____

17 Always strive to make the next CV better. ☐

_____

_____

APPENDIX: PUTTING TOGETHER A CV TO FACILITATE A CHANGE OF CAREER

The challenge facing you as you sit down to the job of putting together a CV for the purpose of effecting a change of career is as follows:

- You need to make it clear that you're seeking to change careers; otherwise someone reading your CV could think you've made a mistake and applied for the wrong job.

- You need to say why you've made the decision to change careers – explain your reasons and show that you're serious.

- You need to say why you feel you're suitable for the new career you've chosen and to identify any transferable areas of skill, experience, job know-how, etc.

- You need to address your salary expectations and make it clear to employers that you accept that, in the short term, your earnings may have to fall.

 COACH'S TIP

Stress the positives

Rather like changing jobs, the reasons for wishing to change career need to come across in a positive framework. In particular, you need to avoid projecting yourself unintentionally as a misfit or someone who is perpetually discontented. The way to do this is to focus at all times on the benefits you see from making the move into your new career. Don't dwell on the negative by listing all the bad points of the career you're in now.

Most of the information that normally goes into a CV will be irrelevant to someone who is considering you for a completely different career, so you will need to give this some thought. The detail about what you did in previous jobs may be interesting up to a point but, if you give it too much exposure, it could act as a turn-off. Because it lacks relevance, it will not act as an incentive to read on.

Similarly, going into raptures about the work you're doing now or the work you've done in the past will strike the reader as paradoxical in someone who is seeking to change careers. At worst, conflicting messages like this can come across as showing lack of commitment.

Let's look at some of the specific sections of your 'change of career' CV.

Personal aims and ambitions

This is the biggest challenge – getting it across in your CV that:

- you are seeking to change careers

- you have good reasons for wanting to change career

- you're serious about it.

What do you need to say? Here is an example:

Aims

I am looking to move into the design, commissioning and installation of mechanical handling equipment. My reasons are as follows:

- I have worked on the maintenance of mechanical handling equipment in a fully automated assembly plant for the last nine years.

- I have served a full mechanical engineering apprenticeship.

- I recently did a mechanical engineering degree in my own time and passed with first-class honours.

- I am seeking to use my experience and qualifications to enter a more challenging field.

The points to pick out from this example are as follows:

- It's clear and concise – no one reading it is left in any doubt that this is someone seeking to move out of a hands-on job into a professional career.

- It's positive – the candidate doesn't air any gripes about still working on the tools.

- It identifies the candidate's transferable talents.

- The fact that the candidate has done a degree in his or her own time shows commitment.

Salary

Many candidates bent on a change of career slip up by putting information about present earnings in their CV and leaving it at that. The signal to anyone reading it is that the candidate is expecting to better, or at least maintain, this level of earnings. Because the candidate is applying for a job as a beginner, this will flag up as a mismatch and the probable outcome is that the candidate's CV will be put on the 'No thank you' pile. Certainly, you should not expect an employer bombarded with applications from eminently suitable candidates to take the time and trouble to ring you up to clarify matters. You are the outsider as far as this particular contest is concerned. The clarification is down to you.

Again, what do you need to say? Here is what our maintenance fitter with the first-class honours degree did to overcome the problem of communicating pay expectations.

Salary

I am currently earning £xx,xxx per annum of which £xxx.xx is made up of shift payments. In seeking to move into a career where I will enjoy better prospects, I recognize that I may have to accept lower earnings at first. Fortunately, my partner is in well-paid employment and in this way we will be able to make up any shortfall.

Points to pick out are as follows:

- Assuming that the job of design, commissioning and installation engineer would mean working normal office times, identifying that an element of the current salary package consists of payments for unsociable hours helps any prospective employer to compare the two jobs on a like-for-like basis. Expressed in this way, the reduction in earnings is not such a big one and this may help to ease some employers' concerns.

- The reference to the partner's well-paid job demonstrates that the candidate has thought through the financial implications of changing careers and made plans accordingly. In this way, it addresses another of the concerns that employers have.

 COACH'S TIP

Be proactive!

Remember that employers don't have to take a chance on you. They can offer the job to someone with a proven track record. See it, therefore, as your job to be proactive and pre-empt employers' concerns. Don't think that the concerns aren't there or, worse still, expect employers to address the issues. In most cases, they won't bother and, really, why should they?

Employment history

Consider the relevance of the information in your CV and don't hesitate to prune out any excess detail in your job history.

A final word of warning

Changing careers isn't easy and typically you run into the brick wall of employers turning you down because of your lack of experience. Here the temptation is to do a bit of tinkering with your CV, with the idea that, if experience is the passport to the jobs, why not invent a little?

Making false claims about previous experience is a dangerous game. Not only do you run the risk of being found out but, more worrying in many ways, your little ruse may succeed. You get the job on the basis of experience that you haven't had, which means that:

- the expectation placed on you to perform will be higher than your true capability
- the normal allowances given to beginners won't be extended to you.

Needless to say, finding yourself out on your ear after six months won't be a very good start to your new career. So, even though you're finding it difficult to get interviews, always be honest with employers. If they decide to give you a chance, let it be on the basis of your limited or non-existent experience. Let them be the ones to decide whether they can live with a learner or not.

HELP DESK

SHORT PERIODS IN JOBS: DOES IT LOOK BAD ON YOUR CV?

'For one reason or another, some of the positions I have held have lasted only for a few months and my concern is that, if I put them on my CV, it could create a bad impression. A suggestion (from a friend) was to leave them off and deal with the gaps in time by tweaking the starting and finishing dates of the other jobs I have had. What do you think?'

Spending short periods of time in jobs would normally be seen by employers as evidence of someone who finds it hard to settle or someone who has failed and got the sack (i.e. unless they're told differently, they assume the worst). Here is perhaps the clue about what to do when it comes to designing a CV. When you have stayed in a job for only a few months, explain why in your reason for leaving. For example, if the job was only a temporary position, then say so. Bear in mind that a few jobs in your track record where you didn't stop long isn't a hanging offence, whereas pulling the wool over an employer's eyes and getting found out is.

BEING TRUTHFUL ABOUT MY SALARY: COULD EMPLOYERS TAKE ADVANTAGE OF ME?

'I have formed the view that I am underpaid for the level of responsibilities I hold and this is the main reason I'm trying to find another job. What bothers me, though, is that, if I follow your advice and put my current salary in my CV, employers will take advantage of me. They will offer me jobs thinking I can be hired for a lower figure than someone who is better paid. What do you think? In my case would it be better to say I'm earning a higher salary?'

What you will be putting in your CV is not just your current salary but also the salary you want to earn in your next job. This should have the effect of stopping short any employer who thinks you can be hired on the cheap. Having said this, the concerns you have voiced are well founded. But don't address them by getting drawn into worrying deceptions. Tell the world that just because you're underpaid now doesn't mean you want to go on being underpaid. Stating your pay expectations clearly and unequivocally is especially important for someone in your position.

WHAT TO READ INTO TURN-DOWNS

'I had a number of experiences where I went for interviews, only to learn when I got there that the salary on offer was way below the figure it would take to tempt me to move. To address this problem, I did as you suggest and redesigned my CV, making it clear that I would only be interested in a job that paid more than the figure I named. Sure enough,

the time-wasting interviews stopped, only to be replaced by a steady stream of turn-down letters. In terms of discouragement, I'm not sure which is worse. Any comments?

Employers who can't afford you won't as a rule be upfront enough to tell you. Instead, what you get in response to the job applications you send in is the usual standard turn-down letter. Our comment is only to agree with you that turn-down letters can be a source of discouragement, though only if you let them be. Here, perhaps, it is important to remind yourself that the reason for not getting on to an interview list is often more to do with the job than it is to do with you. If employers see you as too good, over-qualified, too ambitious or too highly paid, then, as we see it, that's their problem, not yours. Interestingly, what your experience may suggest is that you are well paid for whatever it is you do for a living. This is not intended as a signal to you to abandon your efforts to find another job but rather to make you aware that the task you are asking your CV to perform may be intrinsically difficult.

WHEN IS A CV TOO LONG?

'Is it right that a CV should be three pages of A4 maximum? If my CV is any longer, will it reduce the chances of it being read?'

Not if it's interesting. What, however, is often the case is that CVs more than three pages long don't get read because most of the information in them isn't relevant to the purpose for which they're intended. Apply the test of relevance rigorously to anything you include in a CV. If you do, you will find the length of your CV takes care of itself.

CAN A CV BE TOO SHORT?

'Is it possible for a CV to be too short?'

The answer is yes, demonstrating perhaps that one message that has got through to everyone about designing a CV is the need to keep it concise. Yet, like all good advice, it can be taken too far, resulting in some cases in one-page CVs where conciseness has been achieved either by using ridiculously small fonts or compressing information to such an extent that nothing of interest is left.

NOT WANTING TO REVEAL THE NAME OF YOUR CURRENT EMPLOYER

'I wouldn't want my boss to find out that I am looking for another job and, for this reason, I would rather not put the name of my current employer in my CV. Will this go against me in any way?'

To be fair to most employers, they respect the need for confidentiality when they're dealing with CVs that people have sent in. However, there is the point that, when you send off a CV, you don't know too much about whom it is going to and how much you can trust them to be discreet. So, if you do feel uncomfortable about revealing your employer's name in a document that is going to go into general circulation, then don't do it. Leave a blank space or, better still, write in a short description of your employer's business without giving away their identity (e.g. 'a major retailer of electrical goods'). Will it go against you? Yes, there may be some employers out there who will see it as being unnecessarily cagey; most, however, will understand why.

NO INTERVIEWS – IS MY CV TO BLAME?

'I am currently employed as a languages teacher but, after working in a school for nearly 18 months, I have come to the conclusion that the profession isn't for me and I am now looking for a position outside the world of education (preferably one where I can put my languages skills to use). I have applied for around 20 jobs I have seen advertised but so far I have not succeeded in getting any interviews. Could it be that my CV is at fault? Advice, please.'

Look back to what we said in Chapter 9 about evaluating the performance of your CVs. In your case, the task you want your CV to perform (change career) is one that is intrinsically difficult because you are in competition with people who will have more to offer than you in terms of their experience. You should therefore be measuring the effectiveness of your CV on a different scale to the one you would use if you were applying for jobs in a field where you do have experience.

Our advice? There are many issues to consider when you have your sights set on making a change of career, not just the design of your CV. Indeed, the time may have come to take a long hard look at everything you're doing, by which we mean examine your whole approach, and do this before you send off any more CVs. What certainly seems to be the case is that all your attention so far has been focused on the visible or advertised job market, where competition from people with experience is going to be at its greatest. You may have rather more success from tapping into the invisible market, by:

- sending your CV to a few selected employers – for example, people who operate globally and who may have a need for someone with your language skills
- using your professional network – in this case, making your ambitions known to anyone who would be in a position to put out feelers on your behalf with prospective employers and, if necessary, put in a good word for you.

An appendix at the end of this book has advice on how to put together a CV to facilitate a change of career.

TAKING OVER INTERVIEWS

'I take the point about taking over interviews, but what about interviewers who start the interview by asking you to say a bit about yourself? Isn't this inviting you to take over and, if so, how do you avoid going off on a track they won't find relevant or interesting?'

One measure of a good interview is who does most of the talking. If it's the interviewer then little is accomplished, whereas if it's the interviewee the process offers a good chance of the employer gaining sufficient information on which to base subsequent judgements. Getting you to say a bit about yourself at the start of an interview is a way of (a) getting this process going and (b) taking pressure off the interviewer and giving him or her time to sit back and listen to you give an account of yourself.

How to handle the situation? Keep your account brief. Confine it to a few words about who you are, your key achievements (your bullet points) and why you're interested in the job. Unless you're invited to do so, don't go into a long chronology about the various jobs you've done because this is where you could find the interviewer's attention waning. If the interviewer is interested in what you did ten years ago when you were at Company Q, he or she will ask you.

ASKING EMPLOYERS TO GIVE AN OPINION

'Why not simply ring employers up and ask why you didn't get picked for the interview? In this way, you'll find out pretty quickly whether your CV is to blame for letting you down.'

In a world where the reason for someone not getting a job can go on to become the subject of litigation, don't expect employers to be open and frank with you about why they decided to turn you down. It is far more likely that they will hide behind smokescreens like, 'There were other candidates who were more suitable' or simply avoid taking your call. In short, it doesn't move you forward very far and in some instances the answer you get could set you off on a completely false trail. Also, bear in mind that it's not an employer's job to tell you whether your CV is any good or not, and don't be too surprised if some of them give you a sharp reminder that they're not paid to be careers advisors.

LEAVING JOBS OFF YOUR CV TO MAKE IT LOOK BETTER

'I have not had a lot of luck with my job applications and a consultant at an agency I am registered with made the observation recently that some employers may be put off by the number of jobs I have had. He then went on to suggest I redo my CV and leave off some of the jobs. What do you think?'

Your consultant is not alone in taking the view that a little tweaking of the facts is all part of the game of putting together a good CV. Indeed, we may be in a minority by urging you to exercise caution about saying anything about yourself that cannot be supported by the truth. Why? Because, however you dress it up, the intention is to pull the wool over the eyes of prospective employers, which they won't like if they take you on and then find out that the information you've given them isn't the full story. While some may take a sympathetic view and see it as something they might do themselves if they were in the position of having to find another job, others may see it as a reflection on your character, and here is where the dangers lie.

Our advice would not therefore be to tamper with your CV. Remember, employers do not expect people to be perfect but they do expect honesty. And remember, at the same time, that we're living in an age where employers are inundated by spurious claims of one kind or another, so they're on high alert to watch out for the kinds of people who are prepared to bend the truth a little to suit their own ends.

HAVING YOUR CV PROFESSIONALLY PREPARED

'Bearing in mind the importance of a good CV, wouldn't it be best to spend a little money and have one professionally prepared?'

Anyone who has worked in recruitment will tell you that a professionally prepared CV is quite easy to spot and begs the questions, 'What's wrong with this candidate? Why have they had to get someone else to put their CV together?' Our advice is always to create your own CV. Putting together a good CV isn't rocket science and there is no reason why you shouldn't be able to make just as good a job of it as someone who styles themselves an expert.

OVERSTATING YOUR EXPERIENCE TO GET MORE INTERVIEWS

'My problem is I'm not getting interviews and it has been suggested that my CV could be at fault. As many of the jobs I'm applying for are asking for more experience than I've got, it's also been suggested that I might benefit from overegging some of what I've done. Any thoughts?'

Yes. Don't do it because, even if you do get interviews, sooner or later you'll be found out. The interview count may look better but you still achieve nothing except for a lot of timewasting (yours and the interviewer's). With a CV, always aim to present a true picture of yourself and let employers judge whether you're interview material or not. If there are shortcomings in your experience, don't try to disguise them or leave them out. Some employers will be happy to consider candidates who don't tick all the boxes, and others won't. Incidentally, there are many reasons why candidates don't get interviews and it's not always to do with their CVs.

THE MOST COMMON FAILING

'What in your experience is the most common failing in CVs?'

Surprisingly, perhaps, it's a lack of logical order in the way in which information is presented. CVs that jump about (e.g. from education to employment experience and back to education) are hard to follow and fail the 'one quick read' test that all CVs have to pass if they're going to get any further. Most employers just give up.

ACTION PLAN

Use this space to write in your action plan for the next time you prepare a CV.

_____

_____

_____

_____

_____

_____

_____

_____

_____

_____

_____

_____

_____

_____

_____

_____

_____

_____

_____

_____

_____

_____

_____

_____

_____

_____

_____

_____

_____

_____

_____

_____

_____

_____

COACHING SESSION 69

Revisit Coaching session 1

Go back to Coaching session 1 at the start of the book and do it again. Have your opinions on any of the statements changed?

If they have, note them here, giving your reasons.

_____

_____

_____

_____

_____

INDEX

lack of, 153–4, 202
taking over, 142, 203
invisible job market, 102–3
IT skills, 46

jargon, use of employers', 67
job applications dossiers, 144–5

key matches, 7, 36,
64–7, 174

lack of logical order in CVs, 205
languages, 46
leisure activities, 48
length of CVs, 201

mailshots
aim of, 81
example of, 86–90
making interesting and relevant, 82–4,
85–7
organizing, 91–4
researching employers, 84–5
success and learning from, 94–5
what's in it for you, 82
management of CVs
making changes, 155–6
measuring effectiveness, 153–4
updating information, 156–7
medical history, 41

names
how to address others, 171–2
how to style yourself, 39
nationality, 48
networks, using, 63, 84–5
notice periods, 46–8

'one quick read' test, 9,
85, 193

pages
first/front, 34–7, 66, 141
numbering and naming, 34
pay *see* salary
periods of notice, 46–8
personal statements, 46
photographs, 37–8
presentation, 5–6, 61
professionally prepared CVs, 204

references, 49
relevant information, providing, 64–5, 201

salary, setting out current and expectations, 21,
46, 200, 208–9
salutation, forms of, 171–2
smokers and non-smokers, 42
spellcheckers, 193
strong points, 7, 36, 64–7, 174
structure see framework CVs

three As of successful job hunting, 77
training courses undertaken, 46
turn-downs, 200–201

unemployed status, 48

websites, employers', 63, 84
white space, 33
word-processing software, 33
words, use of employers', 67
writing, clear and concise,
190–93